If God Can Use Me,
What About You?

If God Can Use Me,

What About You?

On the road to fulfilling your God given Purpose

Know this, that God has a plan and a purpose for our lives regardless of what it may feel like, look like, or where we come from.

Written by
EVANGELIST TERETHA J. LOWE

XULON PRESS

Xulon Press
2301 Lucien Way #415
Maitland, FL 32751
407.339.4217
www.xulonpress.com

Paperback ISBN-13: 978-1-6628-1829-5
eBook ISBN-13: 978-1-6628-1830-1

Table of Contents

Dedication

I dedicate this book to my belated parents, Mr. Willie and Mrs. Annie Houston. I thank God for allowing them to be my parents. My mother lived to see the change that took place in my life. Her prayers were answered when I received Jesus Christ in my life.

I also dedicate this book to my loving husband, Kenneth Lowe, for over thirty years of marriage. I can honestly say that he is my mighty man of valor.

Words of Encouragement

My first memory of Sister Lowe was seeing her as a true worshipper. She was dancing and praising God with all of her heart. There was a genuineness about her that made the viewers want to join in the worship. Later, I found her to be an effectual prayer warrior and Sunday school teacher. She and her husband also spearheaded the prison ministry. In this capacity, I found her to be an awesome preacher with such a powerful testimony of the love and grace of God in her life. Just when I thought I knew everything that I needed to know about her, I discovered that she was an actress and an awesome playwright. The Most High God has given this woman so many talents, and I thank God that she is sharing them with the believers and nonbelievers alike. This beautiful sister in Christ is my true friend and confidant. I sincerely say to her, "I love you and my prayer for you is that you continue to prosper and be in health even as your soul prospers.

We both know that your soul is prosperous because it is filled with the Word."

Marion Smith

This is a great story, by the way. Mrs. Lowe, you have a meaty structure of a book. It really illustrates how God turned your ashes into beauty and much, much more. I cannot wait to stand in line and get my signed copy!

Finola Buckley

Foreword
by Prophet Leonard Ford

*P*raise God! Beloved, I want to encourage you to take your time as you read this short, but powerful, book. This is not just another book about someone who had a difficult time in life, but it is a powerful testimony to the unconditional love of God for people of all lifestyles. It is an account of Evangelist Lowe's personal encounter with the loving God that "so loved the world that He gave His only begotten Son, that whosoever believes in him will not perish but have everlasting life" (John 3:16).

She takes the religion out of her book and shows that God is no respecter of person. She also shares that He is able, and He will save to the utmost all those who will come unto Him and make a full commitment to serve Him.

In this book, Evangelist Lowe reminds us that God has provided the answer to all our dilemmas, and that answer is Jesus and a lifelong relationship with Him.

The statement that Jesus made in Matthew 11:28 still stands today. Jesus said, *"Come unto me, all ye that labour and are heavy laden, and I will give you rest."*

Beloved, Jesus wants to give you the same rest that He has given Evangelist Lowe and countless thousands of others around the world. As you listen to her in this book, you will quickly learn that God wants to use you and make your life significant. God has big plans for you.

Peace and Blessings,
Prophet Leonard Ford
We Always Win.

Remember: JESUS WILL PULL YOU THROUGH IF YOU CAN STAND THE PULL!

Acknowledgments

*M*ost importantly and above all others, I thank and praise God for saving me over thirty-nine years ago, and I love Him more and more each day.

I thank God for my husband, Kenneth Lowe. We have been married for over thirty-one years, and he loves me just the way I am; he encourages me to do all that God has called me to do. Kenneth is my number one fan and constructive criticism go-to person. Thank you so much, Kenneth, for your tender loving care that you have shown me over the years.

Bishop Michael Desmuke and I used to work for the same company many years ago. One day I asked him why he was so happy, and he responded by telling me about the Lord and inviting me to his church. He was very persistent. He asked me a second time after my first visit, and that day I was instantly delivered from drugs and alcohol. This turn of events was the beginning of my new life in Jesus Christ. Thank you so much, Bishop Desmuke.

I am appreciative of Elder L. A. and Sister Rosetta Lindsey, the pastor and first lady of one of my former churches, Faith Temple Missionary Baptist Church. Our church was known as the Holy Ghost Headquarters. The reason was that the Word went forth with the anointing and fire of the Holy Ghost. People would say that our church was a Pentecostal church because we gave God praise by dancing, singing, and shouting. God knew where I needed to be when I received Jesus in my life. Elder Lindsey preached the Word of God with a fire that registered in a person's spirit and soul. He made sure that I had a solid foundation, and he let us all know that we needed to know without a shadow of doubt that we were saved. He also informed us that we could not wear a false face on Sunday and live like the devil throughout the week. Elder Lindsey stressed to his congregation that we had to live holy. I thank God for you, Elder Lindsey and Sister Rosetta Lindsey, because you were truly positive examples for our congregation.

Apostle Silas and Dr. Jennifer Johnson are pastors of Full Counsel Metro Church. God allowed my husband and me to be under their pastoral leadership for over twenty-five years. During the time that we attended Full Counsel Metro Church, God used the pastors to speak into our lives in a powerful way. They added on to what we had learned years before; it was just like ever-increasing faith encouraging us to use our own faith more. Apostle Silas and Doctor Jennifer Johnson, I thank God for your belief in us. This belief in us came into fruition when you allowed us to be leaders in the church, sharing the gift with which God has blessed us. Dr. Jennifer, thank you so much for allowing God to use you to awaken a gift in me that was lying dormant.

Another person who has inspired me on my Christian journey is Prophet Leonard Ford. I thank the Lord for such an anointed man of God. Prophet Leonard and Sister Jesse Ford were at Faith Temple when I received Jesus Christ in my life. I really appreciate them for their support and encouragement. Thank you so much, Prophet Ford, for taking the time to write a heartfelt foreword for my book.

I am thankful to have Shelia Alexander as a friend and as my administrative assistant in the ministry of which God has blessed me to be the founder, Lifting Up Jesus Christ Ministries. Sister Shelia has been with the ministry for over two decades and has been a cast member in so many of the productions. Thank you, Sister Shelia, for all of your assistance.

I am so grateful for my mother who prayed diligently for me. Moreover, I am thankful for all the people who have prayed for me and who are continuing to pray for me, people that I know and even the ones that I do not know. Thank you all so very much.

Introduction

$\mathcal{I}$ would like you to go on a journey with me by reading this book. You will be able to see in your imagination the true story of some of the things that took place in my life from elementary school until now. Based on these experiences, I have written this book to encourage you to be all that God has called you to be. He has a plan and purpose for your life, regardless of where you are in life currently. He has thoughts of peace, joy, and happiness for you, and He wants to give you an expected end.

Jeremiah 29:11 says, *"For I know the thoughts that I think toward you, saith the LORD, thoughts of peace, and not of evil, to give you an expected end."*

School was a bittersweet experience for me: I wanted to learn, but there was a blockage where I could not understand several of the things that were being taught. I did not want other children to know. So, I frequently misbehaved at school as a cover-up. In hindsight, I should have been retained at least twice, but I was not. When I was fifteen, I became pregnant with my first child and had her when I was sixteen. In the 1960s, students were not allowed to attend public school while pregnant. A teenage mother had to wait until her baby was a year old before she could attend public school. Therefore, I had to take almost two years off from school before returning.

Once I graduated from high school, I moved to San Francisco, California, thinking that I would have a better life. However, that experience led me down a horrible road of destruction. I became strung out on drugs and alcohol and began doing ungodly things to get a fix or a drink. The devil was using me like a puppet on a string. He had me thinking that I could not function unless I was high, but I was not functioning. I was caught in a vicious trap, needing to be set free.

One day a coworker invited me to church, so on the second invite, I went on August 9, 1981. Hallelujah! I ran down to the altar crying, saying that I was so tired. Jesus instantly set me free from sin, shame and hurt. I am so thankful to God that I am no more like Legion, who lived in a graveyard naked, cutting himself, and crying. He was set free by Jesus, who told Legion to go and tell others what great things the Lord had done for him. You can read the entire account of Legion's story in the bible Mark 5:1–20.

Once God set me free, I not only began telling people about the goodness of God, but I became a living testimony. Looking back over my life, I can say that it is truly a miracle how God instantly delivered me! In this book, you will see how God used me to minister in prisons and on street corners. You will see how a gift that was lying dormant in me was awakened. I was inspired to write several plays and skits, which are listed at the end of this book. I have also produced live stage performances and more, it is all by the grace of God and to His glory; nothing is impossible for Him.

I pray that this book is soul-stirring for you as it strengthens your desire for God to reveal His plan and purpose for your life. Furthermore, I pray that you will always want to do the things that are pleasing to Him. **Now, if God can use me, what about you?**

PART ONE

My Existence before Jesus Christ

CHAPTER 1

God's Love for Us

*I*f the Son of God make you free, you are free indeed. There is no other name under heaven by which man or woman can be saved, except the name of Jesus. I thank my heavenly Father for drawing me in. John 6:44 says, "No man can come to me, except the Father which hath sent me draw him." I am so glad I yielded to God's drawing. Hallelujah!

Looking back over my life, I was indeed a miserable wretch, looking for love in all the wrong places. I was just like the Samaritan woman at the well, looking for acceptance, peace, joy, and happiness. As the scripture goes in the book of John, chapter 4, the woman at the well was engaged in her usual activity, coming to get water. Now, Jesus knew that she would be there at that time, the same as He knows when and where we will be at any given time.

Jesus asked the Samaritan woman for a drink of water, and she answered Him with a definitive statement. She thought that Jesus was like any other Jew. As you know, the Jews had no dealings with the Samaritans. Therefore, the woman indirectly told Jesus to ask His people, but this Jewish man, Jesus, was persistent. He let her know, in no uncertain terms, that the water in the well was allowing her to merely exist and that she would thirst again. He continued by informing her that if she were to drink of the water that He could give her, she would never thirst again. Jesus had whetted her appetite, and she wanted some of that water.

To make a long story short, He told her to go get her husband. The Samaritan woman answered and said she had no husband. He candidly responded to her by telling her that she had answered correctly. He then said to her that she had previously had five husbands and that the man she was currently with was not her husband. She could have been in a relationship with someone else's husband.

She left the well running and witnessing for the Lord, excitedly telling the men of that city to come see a man who told her all about herself.

Before Jesus came into my life, I was engaged in unhealthy relationships with men. Drugs and alcohol bound me, but Jesus instantly delivered me. Hallelujah! I did not go through Alcoholics Anonymous or the

Gyst House, which is a drug rehabilitation center in my hometown of Little Rock, Arkansas. These programs and other rehabilitation centers are helping many people get their lives back on track, but I just decided to come to Jesus just as I was, instead of using a facility. It was not because of me that I did not have to go to those facilities; it was by the grace of God.

There was a void in me, and it could not be filled except by Jesus. He has been and still is, using me for His glory. He is allowing me to do things for His kingdom here on earth, things that I never dreamed I could do or would be doing. I will share more about these things later in the book.

I thank God that He gave me a hunger and thirst for His righteousness and a love for His Word. Romans 12:2 lets us know that we should, "*Be not conformed to this world, but be ye transformed by the renewing of your mind.*" The word **conform** means to behave according to socially acceptable conventions or standards. So being conformed to this world, we hurt people who hurt us. We exchange evil for evil. If we are transformed (changed by praying, reading, studying, meditating on the Word of God, and doing the will of God), we respond differently, the way God wants us to respond.

A prime example is in Matthew 5:44–45a, 44 "*But I say unto you, Love your enemies, bless them that curse you, do good to them that hate you, and pray for them which despitefully use you, and persecute you"; 45a "That ye may be the children of your Father which is in heaven."* According to this scripture, we are not supposed to act like the devil's children at any time. I have missed the mark at times, and I have had to ask God to forgive me, and He did. 1 John 1:9 say, *"If we confess our sins, he is faithful and just to forgive us our sins, and to cleanse us from all unrighteousness."*

As children of God, we must spend time with Him daily, developing our personal relationship with Him, which involves thanking and praising Him. We must also sit quietly before Him, waiting for Him to speak to us. God wants us to be changed day by day into the image of His dear Son Jesus Christ, our Lord. I want you to think about the title of this book, *If God Can Use Me, What about You?* You may already be allowing God to use you. If so, that is great. Continue to perfect what He has called you to do, and do not be surprised if He calls you to add on to what you are already doing. If you ask for directions, He will give you directions and wisdom to go along with it. God wants us to fulfill all that He has called us to do in our lifetime.

Through our lives, people will see that our heavenly Father is the only true and wise God, the one who made the heaven and the earth. He is the God who knows every speckle of dust; He knows every grain of sand in this world. Our heavenly Father knows every star by name, and you know what else? He knows who you are. If there are ten thousand Sharon's in this world and your name is Sharon, He knows which one you are. Our face is engrafted in His hand. We are so precious in the Lord's sight; therefore, we must continuously trust God regardless of whatever may come our way.

Philippians 1:6 says, *"Being confident of this very thing, that he which hath begun a good work in you will perform it until the day of Jesus Christ."* It is such a blessing to know that the Lord knows us; He wants us to have peace that surpasses all understanding while He guides us through life doing His will and completing the work that He has assigned to us.

Even if we go through the valley and face unpleasant situations, God's peace is available to us. I want you to remember that you are fearfully and wonderfully made, and that God has a plan and a fulfilling purpose for your life. Now, if God can use the woman at the well to run through town telling people to come see a man that told her about herself, and if God can use me, a person who previously looked for love in all the wrong places, what about you?

CHAPTER 2

Regardless of Your Background, You Are Loved

I was raised on the east side of Little Rock, which at that time was called the East End. It is a low-income area of Little Rock where we had a neighborhood grocery store, a drug store, and a dry-cleaning business. Can you imagine that? They were all owned by friendly white people, except one, the dry-cleaning service was owned by a black family. We were proud black people. Even though we did not have many nice material things, we took pride in the things that we did have. We knew that our next-door neighbors, our neighbors down the street, and other adults would look after one another's children.

I was the sixth of my parents' seven children, and there were many awkward challenges that took place in our home. When I was nine years old, my parents separated; my mother moved from East 9th Street to a house on Harrington Street, taking us with her. My parents divorced shortly after we moved. Mama never tried to turn us against our father; he would always come to visit us. My father was a calm, gentle, and kind man; he would give a person the shirt off his back to help. However, my father had a problem with alcohol. When he drank, he turned into a different person. When he sobered up, he was back to the kind person that I loved.

I know now that alcoholic demons drove my father to his grave at the age of fifty-two. The devil also tried to destroy me with drugs and alcohol many years ago, but I cried out to Jesus, and He set me free. I will go into more details about that experience later. Now, allow me to get back to my parents. My mother had a lot of spunk and energy. When she saw something that needed to be done, she did it without making excuses. She was very energetic and feisty, which is part of my character with a balance. I also have some of my father's personality, such as a calm, easygoing spirit.

When I was in the first grade, I had a teacher named Mrs. Isom. She was so genuinely nice and kind. She took the time to work with those of us who had a difficult time learning. Mrs. Isom did not make me feel stupid, nor did she intimidate me. I felt a sense of peace while in her room. The second grade was also peaceful with Mrs. Bogart. She spent extra time with her students and made sure that we were learning.

On the contrary, from the third to the sixth grade, I did not learn very much. It would have been better for me if I had been retained a grade or two. That way, I could have maintained the foundation of my elementary school learning. I would not ask for help in the classes because I wanted to cover up the fact that I was not learning. Furthermore, to take the attention off my lack of understanding, I began to act out in class by being a class clown and talking back to the teachers.

I was suspended when I was in the eighth grade. As a result, my mother was required to meet with a reform school representative, who tried to convince her to send me to a reform school for girls. In my mind, I thought that reform schools were for girls who had gotten in trouble for shoplifting and for those who had run away from home. I was so happy when my mother told the representative that she would not send me to a reform school. I felt really good seeing my mother standing up for me.

After a few days of suspension, I went back to school with the same problems of not learning and not asking the teachers or someone questions who could help me.

In May 1965, I completed the tenth grade at Horace Mann High School in Little Rock. Even though we could not afford to go on a family vacation, it was simply good to have a school break. In July of that year, being only fifteen years old, I realized that I was pregnant; I lived in fear being afraid to tell my mother or anyone else what was going on with me. When school opened in September, I was showing a little, but I went back to school for a couple of weeks as if nothing had changed. I was sad, scared, and ashamed.

When my mother learned of my dilemma, she was hurt and saddened, because she wanted me to graduate from high school and possibly go into the Navy as my older sister had done. My mother had to take off from work for a few days to get herself together; afterward, she made doctor's appointments for me to receive prenatal care. She also made arrangements for me to get assistance to pay the hospital bill.

In March 1966, I gave birth to a beautiful eight-and-a-half- pound happy baby girl. Even though school was bittersweet for me, I wanted to go back and finish. In those days in Arkansas, a girl could not return to school until her baby was twelve months old. Therefore, I did not return to school until the fall of 1968. At that point, I attended Central High School and graduated in 1969. My mother was so happy, and so was I.

Regardless of how God allowed you to come into this world (by way of married parents, single parents, adoption, rape, molestation, attempted abortion, or strict Christian parents), you are here, and the Lord loves you. If you are hurting from things in your past or things that are going on in your life now, the Bible lets us know to cast all of our cares over to Jesus because He cares for us. Jesus will give us peace and direction in every situation that may arise in our lives.

To give you a brief summary of Numbers 22, Balak, the king of Moab, was afraid of the Israelites because of how they had overcome the Amorites, and there were so many of them. Balak did not want them on his land where they had settled in the plains. Therefore, he thought if a curse were to be put on the Israelites, it would make it easier for the Moabites to get rid of them. To accomplish this goal, he sent a group of honorable men to inform the prophet Balaam that he, the king, wanted him to curse the Israelites. Balaam advised the men to spend the night at his place and told them that he would take this inquiry before the Lord. The Lord told Balaam not to go to Moab, and that he could not curse the Israelites because they were a blessed people.

Balak then sent more prestigious men to ask Balaam to come and curse the people. Once again, Balaam told the men to spend the night and that he would ask the

Lord. God had already told Balaam no, so why would he ask God again? This scenario reminds me of events with my children when they were growing up. On occasion, they would repeatedly ask me if they could go to a friend's house after I had already told them that they could not go. I would say, "How many times are you going to ask me that same question? The answer is still 'no,' and you had better not ask me again."

On this second time, when Balaam asked the Lord if he should go, God told him that he could go with the men but that he must act on what God tells him to do. God was angry because Balaam persisted after God had initially said "no." Therefore, God arranged for an angel to be in the path as an adversary against Balaam as he traveled on his donkey. However, Balaam did not see the angel, but the donkey did.

As a result of the donkey seeing the angel with a sword drawn, the donkey went into a field to dodge the angel, leading Balaam to hit her. Attempting to avoid the angel again, the donkey ran into a wall and crushed Balaam's foot, so Balaam hit the donkey again. Finally, when there was no way to escape the angel, the donkey fell down and further angered Balaam, causing him to hit the donkey a third time.

The Bible says in Numbers 22:28, *"And the Lord opened the mouth of the ass, and she said unto Balaam,*

What have I done unto thee, that thou has smitten me these three times?" Balaam had an entire conversation with the donkey; he was not even surprised that the donkey was talking back to him. I would have been utterly amazed.

The Lord opened the eyes of Balaam to see the angel with his sword drawn ready to kill Balaam; if the donkey had not stopped and talked with him, Balaam would have died.

The point is that God used the donkey to speak to Balaam, and his life was spared. There are people that God wants us to witness to about Jesus, and if we are obedient to the Lord, many lives could be spared from eternal damnation. If God can use a beaten donkey to talk, and if God can use me with all of my school issues and becoming an unwed mother at sixteen, what about you?

CHAPTER 3

A Different Way of Life

*A*fter I graduated from high school, my daughter and I boarded a Greyhound bus on our way to San Francisco, California. Even though my mother stood by me through the different challenges, she was very strict, and I was ready to get away from her rules and regulations. I thought she was so mean because she would not keep my baby every time I wanted her to. I wanted to hang out or go clubbing with my friends. Now I was going to be on my own, moving in with relatives that seemed to be so cool. Little did I know that the devil was setting me up so he could use me like a puppet on a string. He wanted me to get deep into sin to snuff the life out of me.

However, God intervened. Praise God! He is so good! When I share the things that transpired in my life before I met Jesus, it is not to glorify the devil but to openly expose his tricks and schemes and show how Jesus set me free. The Bible says in John 10:10,

"The thief cometh not, but for to steal, and kill, and to destroy: I am come that they might have life, and that they might have it more abundantly."

My relatives lived in a beautiful home in the suburbs of San Francisco. On the same day that I arrived, I was turned on to marijuana. It made me laugh a lot and relaxed me. It also made me feel like I did not have a care in the world. I became so hungry for junk food after I smoked a joint. It was as if I had a munchie attack, and any kind of food would do. To add to the fuel, my relatives had all types of liquor in their bar and refrigerator.

It was such a great feeling to be away from my mother's house. There was no way that I would have been smoking marijuana or drinking at her house. There were many beliefs for which my mother stood, and I thought those beliefs were old-fashioned because I did not understand at that time. I do understand now, and I realize that she was looking out for my good. The devil had me thinking when I went to California that my new wayward lifestyle would make me happy and complete. However, I found out that changing locations did not change the empty void in my life.

The Bible says in Hebrews 11:25, *"Choosing rather to suffer afflictions with the people of God, than to enjoy the pleasures of sin for a season."* When you are committing a certain type of sin, you do have plea-sure in it. Just remember that the Word of God says in Romans 6:23, *"For the wages of sin is death; but the gift of God is eternal life through Jesus Christ our Lord."* There is a price that a person will pay for sin while here on earth and throughout eternity.

For instance, if a young woman were to steal money from a bank, and if she were caught, she would be tried and found guilty and sent to prison to pay the wage for her sin. If she decides to live the remainder of her life without receiving Jesus as her Lord and Savior, and die without knowing Him, she will go to hell. After judg-ment, she would be tossed into the lake of fire to burn throughout eternity. However, God gave His Son Jesus Christ for the whole world, whom we must receive to have a life worth living here on earth. We also will have life with Him and our heavenly Father throughout eternity. Jesus has already paid the wages of sin for us.

Shortly after I had moved in with my relatives, they taught me how to go to individual clinics to get bar-biturates, which we called downers. We got them and traded them for other drugs, such as speed to keep us hyped. I got on welfare, which provided me with a monthly check and food stamps to help contribute to the household of drugs, alcohol, and food. We also stole clothes to sell to support our lifestyle. Once, we were in this dainty clothing store, gathering items to purchase with a stolen credit card. The cashier rang up the clothes, and one of my relatives handed her the card.

Since it was taking the cashier longer than usual to swipe the card, my relative asked for the card back. However, the cashier would not give her the card. As a result, my relative reached across the counter, grabbed the cashier, punched her in the face, and took the card. The cashier had quietly called the police on us, so we ran out the door. It just so happened that a trolley was passing by, so we hopped on it and rode to the car. We then drove to an area near the Fisherman's Wharf, a nice tourist area in San Francisco, where we went shopping and illegally used another credit. This time everything went smoothly.

Being in California was certainly a big change of life for me. I was going to clubs with my cousin and hanging out dancing and drinking. As a matter of fact, I won a dance contest, getting myself a whopping twenty-five dollars doing the funky chicken with a mixture of other dances. When I went up to get my money, the disc jockey asked where I was from. I told him Arkansas, so he called me T-Red from Arkansas, the T-Red representing the first initial of my name and the tone of my complexion. It was so exciting to me when the crowd joined in on the T-Red chanting. That was a lot of fun then, but now I dance for the Lord, thanking him, praising him, and making a joyful noise before him. My God has turned my mourning to dancing! Hallelujah!

On some Sundays, my cousin and I would go to Hippie Hill, the Golden Gate Park. On one of these occasions, a man came through the park with his entourage. I heard some of the people calling him Jesus, and he was throwing little pills of acid and LSD in the grass. Becoming a part of the hype, I started calling him Jesus, too. He was just smiling. It appeared that he thought he was some type of savior. I thank God that I know the real Jesus now. I took that LSD and began to wildly trip, as the lingo goes.

I started to laugh at everything: people looked funny, their teeth were green, and the list goes on. It seemed as if extra brightness was all over the area. Floors were fading in and out into all different colors. I do not remember how long that high was, but I was ready to go again when it was over. On the contrary, now I am on a Holy Ghost high, having the joy of the Lord, being led in God's path of righteousness, and desiring more and more to be like Him.

We went to Hippie Hill a few more times on Sundays with the expectation of "Jesus" being there throwing LSD in the grass while we attempted to catch as much as we could. He showed up a couple of times while my cousin and I were there.

Years later, I met the one and only Jesus, the savior of the world. He is the Son of the true and living God. He is the one who can deliver anyone who believes in Him. He denied himself and suffered great pain for us all.

When Jesus was carrying the cross to His crucifixion, the Roman soldiers lashed him with a whip that had seven strands of leather with metal on each strand. While the Roman soldiers were beating him, the metal dragged forcefully into His back. Jesus took thirty-nine stripes for us. The Bible says in Isaiah 53:5, "*But he was wounded for our transgressions, he was bruised for our iniquities: the chastisement of our peace was upon him; and with his stripes, we are healed.*"

Jesus took all the ridicule without complaining. A person in the crowd violently pushed a crown of thorns onto His head, causing pain, bloodshed, and bruises. Jesus was pierced in His side, and His arms were stretched out with His hands and feet nailed to the cross. Jesus underwent all of this to redeem mankind back to God.

He broke down that middle wall of partition that separated us from God. Jesus was obedient even unto death, but on the third day after His death, He arose from the grave. The Bible tells us that Jesus let His disciples know in Acts 1:8, *"But ye shall receive power, after that the Holy Ghost is come upon you: and ye shall be witnesses unto me both in Jerusalem, and in all of Judaea, and in Samaria, and unto the uttermost part of the earth."* Start witnessing where you are about our Lord and Savior. This is the real one-and-only Jesus saying this, not the fellow on Hippie Hill. If Jesus can use me, a former thief and party girl, to be a witness for Him, what about you?

CHAPTER 4

A Long Road of Destruction

*L*iving with my relatives began to get old; there was a lot of tension in the house, so I got an apartment in the projects. My apartment had one bedroom and a small sitting area big enough for a couch, lamp table, and television. The sitting room connected to the small kitchen area. The only furniture we had was a loveseat, two mattresses, and a small kitchen table with two chairs. I continued to get high from cocaine, marijuana, red devils (barbiturates), and speed. I had gotten completely out of control. I was not even taking care of my daughter properly, leaving her with relatives and other seemingly decent people I had met in the projects. Sometimes I would even allow her to stay overnight with other people while I was getting high.

Not wanting to face life without being high, I felt like I could not function properly without the drugs and alcohol. Little did I know that I was not functioning properly then. The devil had me blinded, even though I did see the signs of my passing out and other signs when I would come down off a high. I would feel so bad and would sometimes say that I was going to stop.

However, as soon as I found other places to get high with acquaintances and strangers, it was like a magnet drawing me in with no self-control. Sometimes I did not know what I was doing while I was tripping on the drugs and alcohol. The so-called happiness that was there when I first moved to San Francisco was gone. I found myself doing things that I normally would never do to support my habits.

My relatives lost their lovely home, and four of them moved in with me and my daughter. They lived with us for two months in that one-bedroom apartment. I did not mind because they did help me when I first moved there. Once again, we were pooling our money and food stamps to get liquor and drugs. We were "boosting" clothes; that is, selling clothes that we had stolen from ritzy department stores. After my cousin taught me how to wrap clothes around my stomach to the point of looking pregnant, I would have several items of clothing to sell when I left the store. We were on a vicious cycle of destruction; our human reasoning had become very dull.

My mother decided that she wanted to move to California, so her brother and his wife picked out a nice apartment for her. Afterward, my brother and one of his friends loaded up a U-Haul truck and moved her to her apartment in San Francisco. My mother stayed for about two months and was ready to go back home to Arkansas. She asked me if she could take her grand-daughter back with her. I told her that she could, and I was happy that she did. This would allow me to really hang out and be footloose and fancy-free.

One evening while partying, I was involved in a fight, and my tongue was cut off almost an inch. It was hanging on by a mere piece of skin. The frenulum, the thin-looking string underneath my tongue, was gone. I hitchhiked to the emergency room, holding my bleeding tongue in my mouth. My face was all bruised and bloody. The doctor stitched my tongue back together. However, it kept coming loose because of the saliva. During that time, I could only sip broth and could not eat any food. My tongue was swollen for several months, and I could not talk properly, but I kept on getting high, smoking marijuana, drinking vodka, and taking prescription and nonprescription pain pills. After I made several visits to the doctor for check-ups and re-stitching, he told me that it was a miracle that my tongue had finally begun to mend. I was able to eat solid food and talk again, even though it was a slow process.

I have never forgotten those words the doctor spoke, "It's a miracle." Eventually, a new frenulum grew underneath my tongue. I talk better now than I did before that tragic incident. I know now that the devil was trying to shut me up, but God has made me a mouthpiece for Him. I am so thankful to be saved and be a mouthpiece for God.

Since we do not know other people's testimonies, we should not be so quick to judge them. I know that I get radical many times when I am praising God at church and at home. I am not ashamed to praise Him because I can honestly look back over my life and see how the Lord spared my life and took me out of darkness and placed me in His marvelous light with a sound mind. By His grace and mercy, I am not crazy, blind, lame, or dead.

I absolutely know that God had His angels watching over me and protecting me so many times when I was in the world making foolish decisions. Even when I was in places where I could have died, God rescued me. There was a time when I was with three men in a hotel room. We were not having sex but shooting up heroin getting high. They gave me too much and things started getting darker and darker. I was moving in slow motion and stumbling around the room when I fell on the bed. I could hear them talking, but I could not respond. One of them said, "Man, she done OD-ed." In other words, he was saying I had overdosed. Another said, "Let's shoot her up with some cocaine." That was to counteract the heroin and possibly keep me alive. They gave me the cocaine, and they left.

Somehow, I got up off the bed and staggered out of the room, which was on the street level. I do not even remember how I got home. All I can say is that God had His angels watching over me. Hebrews 1:14 says, *"Are they not all ministering spirits, sent forth to minister for them who shall be heirs of salvation?"* Our heavenly Father is so good to us, He has angels watching over us to help us even before and after we are saved. God has His angels encamped around us, which is what it says in Psalm 34:7 *"The angel of the Lord encampeth round about them that fear him, and delivereth them."*

Acts 12:7–11 tells how Peter was bound in jail, and Herod was going to bring him out to be killed, but the saints were praying to God on Peter's behalf. As a result, an angel came and delivered him. This scripture says in verse 7 *"And, behold, the angel of the Lord came upon him, and a light shined in the prison: and he smote Peter on the side, and raised him up, saying, Arise up quickly. And his chains fell off from his hands." 8 "And the angel said unto him, Gird thyself, and bind on thy sandals. And so he did. And he said unto him, Cast thy garment about thee, and follow me." 9 "And he went out, and followed him; and wist not that it was true which was done by the angel; but thought he saw a vision." 10 "When they were past the first and second ward, they came unto the iron gate that leadeth unto the city; which opened to them of his own accord: and they went out, and passed on through one street; and forthwith the angel departed from him." 11 "And when Peter was come to himself, he said, Now I know of a surety, that the Lord hath sent his angel, and hath delivered me out of the hand of Herod, and from all the expectation of the people of the Jews."*

Remember that we have angels to protect us and watch over us. Let us keep them busy. I certainly had my angels busy before Christ and after I received Christ. On August 27, 2020. I was driving on Interstate 430 South, the wind from Hurricane Laura was blowing, and it was raining. I was in the right lane, and there was another car in the center lane, that car swerved and headed toward my lane. I slowed down to give the driver more room just in case she was to venture into my lane.

Suddenly, the car's back bumper hit the left front side of my car near the headlights. I went down a slope sideways as I was saying in my mind, "I'm not staying down here." My radio was playing, and the message in the song resounded over and over in my ears, "Jesus, Jesus, Jesus." I pressed on the gas pedal, and I came back up the side of the slope, parking right behind the car that had swerved.

She got out of her car, asking me if I was okay. I told her that I was. I realized that an angel protected me and guided me up the slope that day. Even though I did not call on the name of Jesus at that moment, His presence was there vividly in the song on the radio, "Jesus, Jesus, Jesus!" Hallelujah! What the devil meant for evil, God turned around and made good. The weapon might have been formed against me, but it did not prosper. The Bible also says in Romans 8:28 "*And we know that all things work together for good to them that love God, to them who are the called according to his purpose.*"

I thank God for His promises. God has people in every walk of life who are called according to His purpose. Some are medical doctors, lawyers, judges, janitors, and stay-at-home mothers and fathers who raise their children while their spouses' work. God also has police officers, teachers, and maids. He has people who are called according to His purpose, which includes alcoholics, former prostitutes, drug addicts, those who did not complete school, and professors who have master's degrees and PhDs. Whatever our occupations may be, let us use them to glorify God and attract more people to His kingdom. Now, if God can use me, a former alcoholic and drug addict, what about you?

CHAPTER 5

Back Home with Baggage

*I*n the latter part of 1971, I left San Francisco three months pregnant with my second child. I decided to come back home to my mother's house. I was so glad to see my mama and my little girl, and they were happy that I was home. Life in the big city was not for me. Even though I was back at home, I brought back bad habits, and I still had a void in my life. The emptiness in my soul needed to be filled with the love of Jesus, but I was not ready for Jesus. I wanted to do my own thing, not realizing that the devil was continuously using me.

In January 1972, my unborn baby's daddy came to Little Rock to marry me. My mother allowed him to live in a separate room until we got married. She did not allow unmarried couples to live together in her home. We were married shortly after he arrived. He found a job, saved his money, and moved us into a nice two-bedroom apartment. At this point, I was not using drugs and alcohol as much as I was in California; however, I was still using them.

My husband, at that time, was a good, hardworking man, providing for his family, but that did not stop me from having a male friend that also liked to get high. When my husband would leave for work, I would call him to pick my baby and me up from the laundromat, which was around the corner from where we lived. While I was spending the day with him getting high, sometimes my husband would have gotten off from work and prepared dinner. I would come home still high and make up a lie that I had been at my friend Linda's house. He would clean up our son, put him to bed, and try to talk with me, but I would have passed out by then. He put up with me running around so many times that he finally went back to California, and I never heard from him again.

I went through many years of looking for love in all the wrong places, leading to a boyfriend beating me with a hammer on the front porch where I used to live. I was not running around with other guys while I was with this particular fellow, but he was "crazy" and controlling. I finally left him. During that time, I worked at a liquor warehouse. What a great place to work to support my drinking habit, so I thought. Of course, this was another setup by the devil. At times, the supervisor allowed the workers to buy boxes of liquor for a minimum amount of money. I had a liquor store in my car, so to speak. When people heard about it, selling liquor from my car became a part-time job for me. I was drinking as much as I wanted, but that eventually came to an end.

My friend Linda and I were at a club one night, and in walked Ben Dodd and his cousin. I did not know who Ben was at that time, but I liked the way he looked. I thought he would talk with Linda because I felt she was prettier than I was. However, he walked directly over to me, and I was so thrilled. We began dating and remained a couple for seven years. During that time, we had a child, which was my third one.

I wanted Ben to marry me, but he would not. One time I thought he had stolen my money, so when he was asleep, I took a lamp and hit him on his forehead. I later learned that he had not stolen my money; I had hidden it from myself. That scar was with him for the rest of his life. We had a lot of ups and downs during our time together. The stolen money allegation was just one of them.

In July 1981, Ben and I went to his hometown to visit his friends in Batesville, Arkansas. I was sitting in a swinging chair smoking a joint while looking around the room and seeing others getting high on heroin. A young man asked me if I wanted a "fix." I told him no. I was saying to myself, "God, I am so tired of living life this way." I knew that my mother was praying for me, and people I did not even know were praying for me.

I say that because since I have been saved, I also pray for people who may not know Jesus in the pardon of their sins. Some of the ones that I pray for do not know me. I pray that laborers will come across their paths and witness to them about Jesus Christ's saving power and that they will want to know Jesus. I pray this prayer for people I know and for those that I do not know. As stated in 1 Timothy 2:1, *"I exhort therefore, that, first of all, supplications, prayers, intercessions, and giving of thanks, be made for all men."* This scripture tells us to pray and give thanks for all people, not just for those who know Jesus, but also for those who do not.

When I was sitting in that swinging chair in Batesville saying to myself, "God, I am so tired of living life this way," I had gotten tired of the drugs, alcohol, and the wild lifestyle that came with it. This lifestyle involved having a wreck, hitting a telephone pole, and flipping the car upside down, all while I was seven months pregnant with one of my children. Neither my baby nor I was hurt in this accident. Praise God!

Another incident that proved God's grace and mercy were with me was when I found out that Ben was dating another woman while we were together. A friend of mine's allowed me to use her gun to shoot the other woman. However, while we stood in the alley waiting to see if she would come to the Diplomat Club, the gun literally fell apart in my hand; it started dropping to the ground piece by piece.

Looking back, I am so glad that my planned crime did not happen, it wasn't the other woman's fault. I should have gotten Ben out of my life much earlier since I was tired of being unhappy, lonely, and lost. I did not realize that all of the things I had suffered and the acts I had committed were about to be wiped away. They were about to come to an end by the precious blood of Jesus. Little did I know that God was in the process of drawing me to Him. The Bible says in John 6:44a, *"No man can come to me, except the Father which hath sent me draw him."*

I had cried out to God many times; this time, my heart must have been different. God was drawing me to him, and I could feel it. The Bible says in Jeremiah 31:3, *"The Lord hath appeared of old unto me, saying, Yea, I have loved thee with an everlasting love: therefore, with loving kindness have I drawn thee."* God is not only talking to Jeremiah in this passage of scripture; He is also talking to us. He loves us with a type of love that no one else can give, and nothing or no one can compare to His kindness toward us.

Two weeks before I surrendered to Jesus, I was at work, sad and needing answers to why I could not get my life together. I was able to go two weeks at a time without getting high, but I would make up for that two weeks in three days when I started back with the drugs and alcohol. I wanted to stop, but I simply did not have the will power to do so. One day when I was at work, one of my coworkers was singing church songs, and I asked him what he was so happy about. He said, "Well, T, I truly know the Lord now. I have been singing about Him, but I really didn't know Him at first; He has given me so much joy."

Then he asked me to visit his church. I did not want to go, but I thought that if I went this one time, he would not ask me again. So, I went the following Sunday to an evening service. The choir sang, the preacher preached, and the deacons prepared to serve the Lord's Supper. I felt that I was not supposed to partake of the Lord's Supper because of the way I was living, so my children and I left. The next day my coworker asked why I had left early. He had wanted to introduce me to his pastor.

He asked me to visit the next Sunday. All kinds of thoughts were running through my mind because I did not want to go back. I was thinking, "I don't have anything to wear. I can't wear the same dress I wore the other Sunday because people will be talking about me." Even so, I told him that I would be there. It worked out that I was in the right place at the right time. God had set me up to be delivered. Unknowing to me, the following Sunday would be the Sunday that I would be delivered from sin, shame, drugs, alcohol, and illicit sex.

The day before that Sunday, I was still trying to figure out where I could get another dress. I had about eight dollars, and that was not enough to buy a dress. Let me tell you that God had already worked it out while I was trying to figure it out. That Saturday, I was driving home on Lew Drive, headed toward Lew Circle, which is where I lived at that time. I came to a stop sign and saw a rummage sale sign pointing to the left. I went there and found five dresses, and they were nice dresses, for only five dollars.

On Sunday morning, my children and I went to church. I do not recall what was preached but after his sermon, I remember the preacher saying, "The doors of the church are open. Will you come?" I began to have mind battles, thinking that if I were to go down there, everyone would be looking at me. I said to myself, "If someone else goes, I will go." The pastor kept saying, "Will you come?" A lady stood up on the other side of the room, and I ran up there crying and saying, "I'm tired! I'm tired! I am so tired!" I was not thinking about anyone else in the room. (My eyes are tearing up even now as I write about that day.)

The pastor said, "Wonderful, wonderful Jesus." He asked me to give my name, and I did so. Then I pointed toward my three children and identified them. I went on to tell him that I smoked dope. I said it in front of everyone, and the pastor kept saying, "Wonderful, wonderful Jesus." I do not remember a prayer of salvation or deliverance. I do remember the congregation singing the song, "I Have Decided to Follow Jesus and No Turning Back." That was thirty-nine years ago. That second Sunday in August 1981 was the day that I made the best decision of my entire life.

Mark 5:1–20 talks about a man named Legion. He had two thousand demons aggravating him and tormenting him so much that he lived in the graveyard. People tried to bind him with chains, but he broke loose. Those demons had pushed him to the point of cutting himself, crying, and bleeding night and day. The scripture does not say he was bleeding, but typically if you are cut, blood is present. In other words, this man was miserable because the demons were causing him to abuse himself. Of course, he did not like being in that situation.

I used to be like Legion in the graveyard, cutting myself with different vices of the world. I was bound with chains, a slave to sin. Some of you may be in the same condition with other circumstances. For instance, you may be leaving your happy home for another man or woman, or you may be gambling all your money away and not taking care of your family. You may have such a strong drive to build a business or a career that nothing else matters. You may not realize that what you feel you need at this moment could be a trick of the devil.

One day when Jesus came into town, the unclean spirits in Legion saw Him and ran to Jesus, pretending to worship Him. Jesus told the unclean spirits to come out of the man called Legion. We must be aware that demonic spirits can operate in a person even when that person appears to be a saint. We must call these evil spirits out and set people free in the name of Jesus. Once Legion was set free, the Bible says that others saw him sitting, clothed, and in his right mind. When Jesus got ready to leave, the man that used to be full of the devil wanted to go with Jesus. The Lord told him to go home and to his friends and tell them the great things the Lord had done for him.

God used a young man on my job, Brother Michael Desmuke, to witness to me. He was persistent in inviting me to church, where I surrendered all to Jesus. I will be ever so grateful to him for allowing God to use him to lead me to Jesus. Now if God can use a demon-possessed man to witness for Him, and if He can use Brother Michael Desmuke to witness to me and lead me to church to receive Christ, a use to be adulterer, what about you?

PART TWO

My Life after Jesus Christ

CHAPTER 6

Walking in the Newness of Life with a Lot of Mistakes

When I arrived home from church, I told Ben that I had been saved, and that we could not live together in sin anymore. I told him that I was going to be baptized on the first Sunday night of the following month. He proceeded to tell me that we could be baptized together. I told him that it did not work that way and that he had to ask Jesus to come into his life. He made the decision to wait awhile. I allowed him to sleep on the living room sofa for about a month until he found a room across town. He did not make any trips to my bedroom during that time, and I did not make any trips to the living room sofa. He tried to hug me once, but I told him that we could not do that, and I moved away.

I felt that if I were to hug him, it would lead him on to expect something more than I was willing to give. I had made up my mind. However, we had Bible study together during that time, and even after he got his own place, Ben would go to church every Sunday with me. That really made me feel good. I occasionally invited him over for Sunday dinner, and he was the perfect gentleman. I was so happy. It looked like everything was coming together.

To make things even better, I was teaching my children the Word of God. My two oldest children were excited about telling my mother that I had gotten saved and did not drink anymore. I was so thankful not to be bound any longer. Whenever I used to testify about God saving me, I always cried because I would think of how Jesus had instantly delivered me and set me free from the grips of the devil. I had finally gotten tired of the devil using me like a puppet on a string. It was as if I had been stuck in quicksand, going down not to rise again. But Jesus delivered me.

He put a new song in my heart. Rather than singing the blues, I sing praises to Him. Jesus placed my feet on a solid rock and established my goings. The places to which I previously went, I did not go anymore. Every time the church doors were open, my children and I were right there. The Bible says in Psalm 40:1–3, 1 "I waited patiently for the Lord; and he inclined unto me, and heard my cry." 2 *"He brought me up also out of an horrible pit, out of the miry clay, and set my feet upon a rock, and established my goings." 3 "And he hath put a new song in my mouth, even praise unto our God: many shall see it, and fear, and shall trust in the Lord."*

God had truly delivered me, but I was still smoking cigarettes. I went through the phase of throwing packs of cigarettes away. I felt that smoking cigarettes was wrong because the Bible says to abstain from all appearances of evil. However, in the 1980s, employees could smoke at the workplace, in the restrooms, and in the breakroom. One day while I was on my break, I sat on a bench in the restroom and began reading my Bible and smoking a cigarette. I heard a voice in my mind say, "Your body is the temple of the Holy Ghost."

I did not remember reading that scripture at any time, but a spirit of conviction came upon me. I put that cigarette out and have not had another one since. Thanks be to God! I became free from smoking cigarettes about a month after I was saved. I was so happy to be delivered from that habit. I do not know why I was not delivered from smoking cigarettes at the same time that I was delivered from drugs and alcohol, but God knows. Nevertheless, I thank God that I am free!

Everyone at work could truly see the change that had taken place in my life. They no longer saw the old Teretha who used to come to work high on drugs. The old Teretha would sometimes lie down and pass out on cardboard in the warehouse when I was supposed to have been cleaning up. Another time was when my responsibilities were to catch muffins on the muffin line, put them in bags, and place them back on the line to complete the process. When I was high and swaying back and forth, the colored muffin bags looked like fire coming down the assembly line. It was so bad on one occasion, that the supervisor sent me home because I was not able to perform my duties.

I was deeply under the influence for three days, so I mustered up enough nerve to call my supervisor to ask him if I still had a job. He said, "Yes, you do, Teretha. Can you be at work in the morning?" I said, "Yes sir! I'll be there. Thank you." My coworkers noticed how the supervisor allowed me to come back to work, still doing the same old thing. My supervisor and my coworkers were fully aware of the habits of the old Teretha. However, they all saw the tremendous change that was taking place in me. Ephesians 2:8 says, "*For by grace are ye saved through faith; and that not of yourselves: it is a gift of God.*"

However, not everything changed overnight since I was a babe in Christ. An example is that I cursed someone out about something that was none of my business. Pat, the person that I had cursed, said to me, "I knew you were not saved." When she said that, I felt so hurt. Those words stayed with me. I had let my Lord and Savior down, just acting a plumb fool. The next day was my off day, so I went to my job to apologize to Pat and asked her to forgive me. I was honestly sorry for cursing at her. She accepted my apology and said that she believed that I was saved and that it took a real woman to come and apologize. I was so thankful that she had forgiven me.

One Sunday, Pastor Lindsey, who was my pastor at the time, said, "The doors of the church are open. Will you come?" Ben went down and sat in one of those chairs that the deacons usually place in front of the altar. He supposedly received Jesus Christ in his life. I was excited and did not know that the devil was setting me up again. We got married in October 1981. It felt so good to go to church as a family and study the Word of God together.

In November of that same year, Ben gradually stopped going to church, and his old habits reappeared. One Sunday, my children and I came home from church to find Ben drinking beer and smoking a cigarette. I confronted him and said, "You tricked me." He started to go upstairs, all the while smoking his cigarette with his beer bottle in his hand. He gave me such a cold look that he did not even look like my husband. The words that came out of his mouth were, "That was the only way I could keep you." It was like the devil himself was speaking through him to me.

Before I was saved, we "shacked up" for seven years. I did not know that the phrase "shacked up" was in the online Merriam-Webster dictionary until I was writing this book. I thought it was a slang term, but the term has been around since 1935. It means "to sleep or live together as an unmarried couple." Ben did not want to get married during that time, and it seemed as if the devil was using him to be a stumbling block for me. I should have waited to make sure before I married Ben.

The Scripture says in 2 Corinthians 6:14, *"Be ye not unequally yoked together with unbelievers: for what fellowship hath righteousness with unrighteousness? and what communion hath light with darkness?"* So please, ladies and gentlemen, wait on the Lord, and He will strengthen your heart and allow the right person to come into your life. By not waiting, I married a person that during that time had nothing in common with me except for our son. For instance, he wanted to go clubbing, and he did; I did not want to do that anymore.

For seven years of marriage, I never knew how much money Ben made. He would give me a small amount, and sometimes he would not give me anything for the household budget. However, I made sure that the bills were paid because I was trying to be a good Christian wife and making sure me, and my children had a place to stay. I continued to pray that things would change and that he would truly give his life to Jesus. Sometimes Ben would be gone three days at a time and would tell me that he was hanging out and getting high with his cousin. He told me that he was not with a woman. Even though I did not believe that I let it go.

Once when we had gotten into an argument, I took the house key off his keychain while he was not paying attention. When he came home and knocked on the door, I did not let him in. He then went down the street to a phone booth and called a local pastor and his wife. He had heard me listening to this pastor on the radio. When he knocked on the door again, he told me that the pastor and his wife were with him. I was thinking, "What!"

I did not appreciate them coming to my house to try to conduct marriage counseling at almost two o'clock in the morning. I do not remember all they said, but there is one thing I do remember: They told me,

"You need to be obedient to your husband, regardless of what he asks you to do." I asked them if I should go to a club if he were to ask me to go. They said yes. Then I knew that the counseling session was over.

In 1 Thessalonians 5:22, the Scripture says, "*Abstain from all appearance of evil.*" In my opinion, I would truly be misrepresenting Jesus by sitting in a club and doing what my husband (at the time) wanted me to do. The Bible says in 2 Timothy 2:15, "*Study to shew thyself approved unto God, a workman that needeth not to be ashamed, rightly dividing the word of truth.*"

I thank God that I was, and still am, in the Word of God. I knew that was not right what those pastors were saying. That is just like saying if my husband wanted me to jump into the Arkansas River with him, I should do so. I think we all know that this would not happen. Even though Ben was heavy on drugs and alcohol, he never tried to stop me from serving the Lord, nor did he try to stop me from going to church during our time of marriage.

One day I decided to look inside his wallet, which I had never done before. To my surprise, I saw a woman's picture and a condom. Based on the evidence, I did not need a junior high education to know what was going on. The protection certainly was not for me because my tubes were tied, and I did not have any type of venereal diseases. He tried to explain, but my feelings for him were gone, and I did not want to hear his attempts to appease me with his lies. He thought that we would make up as we had done so many times before. However, this time it was over. He contested the divorce, but the judge granted it anyway, and I kept right on praising God. Now, if God can use me, a person who made wrong decisions and ended up in divorce court, what about you?

CHAPTER 7

Getting a Solid Foundation

I thank God for Elder Lindsey and Sister Lindsey, the founders of Faith Temple Missionary Baptist Church, for being where God had appointed them to be. They helped me to get rooted and grounded in the Word of God. Elder Lindsey preached holiness-or-hell sermons. He reminded us of the adage, "Why buy the cow when you can get the milk for free." He would also say, "You need to stop that shacking up and get married; if that man can buy a dog tag for his dog, lady, why can't he go to the courthouse and get a license for you and him to get married?" Elder Lindsey had the anointing of God to destroy yokes and remove burdens. Isaiah 10:27 says, "*And it shall come to pass in that day, that his burden shall be taken away from off thy shoulder, and his yoke from off thy neck, and the yoke shall be destroyed because of the anointing.*"

During that time, many people were saved, set free, delivered, and married in the ministry of Elder Lindsey. God knew what type of ministry I needed to be involved in, and this was where I received a solid foundation. There are scriptures in the Bible about building your house on a rock, a solid foundation and about building a house on sinking sand. In Matthew 7:24-27,

> *"Therefore whosoever heareth these sayings of mine, and doeth them, I will liken him unto a wise man, which built his house upon a rock:" 25 "And the rain descended, and the floods came, and the winds blew, and beat upon that house; and it fell not: for it was founded upon a rock." 26 "And every one that heareth these sayings of mine, and doeth them not, shall be likened unto a foolish man, which built his house upon the sand:" 27 "And the rain descended, and the floods came, and the winds blew, and beat upon that house; and it fell: and great was the fall of it."*

Jesus said if we do these things, we would be like a wise man or woman who built his or her house on a rock, and that rock is Jesus. When the storms of life come in with the rain, wind, and flood, Jesus is our solid rock. The storms of life will not wash us away even though they attempt to harm us. Know that when the enemy comes in like a flood, the Spirit of the Lord will lift up a standard against that enemy.

This standard is His Word that is in our heart and in our mouth where we can speak to every situation that may arise in our lives. When we speak to the negative situations in the name of Jesus, they will have to dry up and cease to exist. I have heard a few ministers say that the comma is in the wrong place in Isaiah 59:19b says, *"When the enemy shall come in like a flood, the Spirit of the Lord shall lift up a standard against him."* These ministers suggest that the comma should be placed after "in," instead of after "flood." They believe the Scripture should read as follows: "like a flood the Spirit of the Lord will lift up a standard."

I suggest that we leave that comma just where it is because it shows how the devil can come against us with everything he has. I believe this scripture is saying that the enemy comes in like a flood. He can have several things happening to us at the same time, trying to wear us out. If we have the Word of God in our hearts, we can speak it out of our mouths to every situation like a force of a machine gun, and the devil will leave running. The Bible also says that if we hear the words of Jesus and do not act on them, we will be foolish men or women who build our houses on sand. Given this situation, when the storms of life come with the wind and rain, we will not be able to stand. Therefore, let us stay anchored in the Lord on that solid rock.

While I was under the leadership of Elder and Sister Lindsey, God was also filling me with His peace and love for others. I wanted God more than I wanted anything else, and I wanted other people to get to know Him. One day I started praying that God would send me Christian friends, and He did. I was so thankful that I met several sisters in the Lord during this process.

Most of us attended the same church, and we all had a kindred spirit. We had prayer and Bible study at one another's homes, and we grew in the Lord. Sister Deborah Thomas was, and still is, a powerful prayer warrior. I asked God to teach me how to pray like her, and He did. That was not a selfish act, nor was I comparing myself to her. I simply wanted to pray to God effectively, and she was a good example.

One of Jesus's disciples asked Him to teach them how to pray. Luke 11:1 says, "*And it came to pass, that, as he was praying in a certain place, when he ceased, one of his disciples said unto him, Lord, teach us to pray, as John also taught his disciples.*" I learned how to use God's Word to pray in every situation. It did not happen overnight, but by the grace of God and by my application in the Word, it happened and is still happening.

Our prayer band started going to hospitals and nursing homes praying for people. One day I was on my way to the nursing home to visit with the elderly when my four-year-old son, who was with me at the time, began to cough constantly. I was thinking, "I wish that he would stop coughing." As I was driving, I could see him out of the corner of my eye looking at me, waiting for me to pray for him. All of a sudden, he said, "Jesus! heal me!" I got into spiritual gear and started praying. Jesus did heal him. I thank God for having had the opportunity to teach my children the Word of God, the power of prayer and how to pray.

There was a time when I was with one of my prayer band sisters, Mozetta Perry, we were so fired up on our way to a revival singing about prayer and obeying God. Whatever He wanted us to do, we were going to obey.

Right after we arrived at the church and sat down, a woman came and asked me if I would pray. I said, "Not at this time." I allowed fear to come upon me. The same woman asked Sister Mozetta Perry, and she prayed. I could not get my heart into the service because I was thinking about how I had sung about obeying God. Then when I was put to the test, I declined. I felt that I had let the Lord and myself down. I said to myself that this would never happen again and that I would be ready next time anyone asked me to pray.

Later, I was faced with another opportunity to pray. One of my friend's sister had a baby, and something was wrong with the baby's health. My friend wanted me to go to the hospital and pray for the baby. When I arrived and asked to see the baby, I discovered that she had died. I saw the little baby all covered up, and I started praying to God to raise the baby up. I began speaking life to the baby, and that was provoking the nurses and was asked to leave. I was taking God at His word and still am. Matthew 10:8 says, *"Heal the sick, cleanse the lepers, raise the dead, cast out devils: freely ye have received, freely give."*

Moreover, Mark 16:17–18 says, 17 *"And these signs shall follow them that believe; In my name shall they cast out devils; they speak with new tongue,"* 18 *"They shall take up serpents; and if they drink any deadly thing, it shall not hurt them; they shall lay hands on the sick, and they shall recover."* I am grateful to have had people in my life to help me grow in the Lord. Prophet Leonard Ford, Evangelist Roosevelt Wilson, and Sister Linda Wilson encouraged me so much during that time in my life.

They were glad to share their knowledge and wisdom of the Lord with me. Prophet Ford held tent revivals in the summertime, and people were saved, set free, delivered, and healed. I remember once when we were at a tent revival on High Street, as Prophet Ford was preaching, a man came in with a gun. Prophet Ford kept on preaching under the anointing of the Holy Ghost.

Another sister and I approached the man, we got on each side of him, and started praying in tongues. As the man walked back and forth, the sister and I walked with him and kept praying. He said to Prophet Ford, "Man, get these women away from me," and he hurriedly left the tent. If this man had chosen to do so, he could have been delivered because the anointing was there to destroy every yoke.

I used to go to many of Prophet Ford's revivals, and I always left encouraged and with more faith. He would sometimes allow me to express encouraging words the meetings for about five to ten minutes. These words not only encouraged the people attending the meeting, but they also encouraged me. I was so thankful that God was using me. Now, if God can use me to pray and encourage others, what about you?

CHAPTER 8

Growing in Grace with My Children

I thank the Lord for giving me a mind to seek Him and want to know Him and please Him. The Lord gave me a mind also to establish my prayer time with Him, which was early in the morning. I read and studied my Bible and listened to a variety of ministers on the radio and television. There were ministers in Arkansas that Sister Perry and I would go to visit, and we would have a hallelujah, foot-stomping time in those services. There were also times of teaching, deliverance, and rebuking. It was such a blessing to us.

Our spirits would let us know when someone was not speaking the true Word of God. We knew if they had twisted the Word to mean what they wanted it to mean. If what was said did not line up with the true Word, we let it go in one ear and come out of the other.

I am so thankful that God gave me another chance to love my children and to train them in the right way. The Bible says in

Proverbs 22:6, *"Train up a child in the way he should go: and when he is old, he will not depart from it."* The Passion Translation (TPT) of Proverbs 22:6 explains this concept in a way that even a child can understand. It says, *"Dedicate your children to God and point them in the way that they should go, and the values they've learned from you will be with them for life."* Even if they try to get away from what they have been taught, it will remain in them when they grow up or mature. Then one day, it will come alive in them. We must continue to pray for our children to receive Jesus Christ regardless of the lifestyle they have chosen to live.

When I gave my life to the Lord, my children saw the positive difference that Jesus made in my daily walk. For example, I was not drinking, doing drugs, or leaving them home alone anymore. I took them to church all the time, and it seems like every time the church doors swung open, we swung in. We made our rounds to revivals indoors and outdoors throughout the years. Now I did take time to make sure they had a balance in their lives, we would go to parks and have a wonderful time throwing frisbees and other things. Once we drove, to Memphis and spent a night at the

Hampton Inn. My mother was with us, so we brought snacks and food to cook in the hotel. Mama had brought some pork chops, cooking grease, a skillet, and a hot plate. Those pork chops were smelling and the smoke start going up to the smoke detector alarm went off, were fanning the smoke away from the detector but it was too much. A hotel worker knocks on the door, we explain to him what happen, and he told us that we could not cook in the room. This incident was funny and serious at the same time. The children really had a good time laughing at what happened, but the pork chops were good. My mother and I never did cook in any more hotels; we had learned our lesson.

There was a time that God instructed me to have my children read Proverbs 3 early in the morning. On one of the days when it was my middle child's turn to read, I just so happened to look up to see that he had his hand under his chin with his eyes closed and was quoting the scripture by memory. Afterward, my youngest son also started quoting the scripture. He got more than halfway through the passage by memory. That blessed my heart so much to see them quoting the Word of God. After my daughter, my firstborn, grew up and left home, she wrote me letters thanking me for not allowing her to do what she wanted to do while growing up. Those were encouraging words that really lifted my spirit.

I took the time to teach my children by the Word of God and by example. I pointed them in the way that they should go, and I know that God allowed me to raise them on a solid foundation. When we invest in our children, that is one of the most powerful things that we can do for our heavenly Father, our children, and ourselves. We must not beat ourselves up if some of them decide to live contrary to how they were raised. Let's thank and praise God, for the Word that has been planted in them will come alive, and they will be changed from the inside to the outside. We must not call things as they are, but as they will be, and speaking into our children's lives whenever the Holy Ghost prompts us. Please remember that we are not to live our children's lives for them. They must live their own lives, and we must continue to pray. Now, If God can use me, a former deadbeat mom, to teach and raise my children the way they should go in the Lord, what about you?

There was a time that God instructed me to have my children read Proverbs 3 early in the morning. On one of the days when it was my middle child's turn to read, I just so happened to look up to see that he had his hand under his chin with his eyes closed and was quoting the scripture by memory. Afterward, my youngest son also started quoting the scripture. He got more than halfway through the passage by memory. That blessed my heart so much to see them quoting the Word of God. After my daughter, my firstborn, grew up and left home, she wrote me letters thanking me for not allowing her to do what she wanted

to do while growing up. Those were encouraging words that really lifted my spirit.

I took the time to teach my children by the Word of God and by example. I pointed them in the way that they should go, and I know that God allowed me to raise them on a solid foundation. When we invest in our children, that is one of the most powerful things that we can do for our heavenly Father, our children, and ourselves. We must not beat ourselves up if some of them decide to live contrary to how they were raised. Let's thank and praise God, for the Word that has been planted in them will come alive, and they will be changed from the inside to the outside. We must not call things as they are, but as they will be, and speaking into our children's lives whenever the Holy Ghost prompts us. Please remember that we are not to live our children's lives for them. They must live their own lives, and we must continue to pray.

Now, If God can use me, a former deadbeat mom, to teach and raise my children the way they should go in the Lord, what about you?

CHAPTER 9

Taking Jesus to the Streets

*I*n the late 1980s, I started a street ministry. I saved my money and went to Radio Shack to buy a PA system and microphone that was designed to use power from the car cigarette lighter. I used one of my speakers from my home so our street ministry team could be heard in a large area surrounding us.

We had pamphlets to give out. One of the pamphlets had a black background with gold flames. It had written on it, "Where will you spend eternity?" The inside of the pamphlet included information about heaven and hell and about making the right choice. The plan of salvation was also explained. I started the street ministry and Sister Perry joined in with me; a few brothers also became part of the ministry.

We traveled to different areas of Little Rock and North Little Rock preaching the gospel. We ministered at Granite Mountain, the East End where I was born and raised, College Station, Highland Park, the corner of Wright Avenue and High Street, and Hemlock Court. A sister asked me if I was afraid to go to those types of places because none of them were on the better side of town. I told her, "No. I used to go to those places when I was not saved. I have the Holy Ghost now, so why should I be afraid?"

In 1 John 4:4, the scripture says, "*Ye are of God, little children, and have overcome them: because greater is he that is in you, than he that is in the world.*" We are victorious through Christ Jesus; remember to stay connected to Jesus. That is where our strength come from.

There was a time when we were preaching at Hollingworth Projects, which used to be in the East End. The people were sitting out enjoying the nice summer afternoon as we sang a few songs and prayed. I told them about Jesus and explained how God had sent Jesus to redeem mankind. I asked the people if they were ready to meet their maker. I told them that a stray bullet does not have a name on it and that somebody could come that day and start shooting a gun. I went on to add that if the bullet were to hit a person and that person were to go to hell, then it would be too late to ask God for mercy.

I gave the microphone to one of the brothers, and he began to talk about the Lord. Afterward, I started talking to a family that was sitting on the porch. Suddenly, it was as though God allowed an instant panoramic replay of what I had just told the crowd. A man came from out of nowhere with a gun, and all the people ran inside their homes in fear of being shot. The man looked at me and said, "I am going to shoot you." As my team stood watching and praying, I went to the microphone and said, "Do you see what I was saying? A stray bullet does not have a name on it."

We continued to preach Jesus, and the man walked away. The Bible says in 2 Timothy 1:7, *"For God hath not given us the spirit of fear; but of power, and of love, and of a sound mind."* Similarly, Psalm 56:4 says, *"In God I will praise his word, in God I have put my trust; I will not fear what flesh can do unto me."* God wants us to put all our trust in Him because He loves us. He is our shield and buckler. In other words, He is our protection.

On one Saturday afternoon, we were on the corner of East 6th and Harrington Streets preaching about Jesus. A man driving a J.B. Hunt truck parked, got out of the truck, and walked over to listen to us. When I asked if anyone wanted to receive Jesus, he came over and accepted Jesus as his Lord and Savior. A year later when we were in the same place, he came by again, got out of his truck, and told us that he was still saved. Hallelujah! God is so good!

Years ago, MacArthur Park used to be a place people would drive through while drinking and smoking dope. The police finally put a stop to that, and the city restructured the park. Some of the streets became beautiful flower gardens and a gazebo was also placed in the park. Years later Sister Perry and I went to the park, walking up and down the sidewalk on the main street in front of the park. I was wearing a sign that read, "I am a fool for Christ" on the front. When people read the front, they laughed until they read the back, which was not so funny. It said, "Whose fool are you?" I tell you that it was a thought-provoking question. I had gotten this idea from a powerful preacher by the name of R. W. Schambach. As 1 Corinthians 4:10 states, "We are fools for Christ's sake, but ye are wise in Christ; we are weak, but ye are strong; ye are honourable, but we are despised."

Paul and others were considered as fools because they were sold out to Jesus. The Corinthians knew the Word of God, but they were not living the Word. They wanted to be looked upon as great philosophers. It is the same way today in some churches. If a person has a notable social position (such as a doctor, lawyer, or prosperous businessperson), that person may know the Word from Genesis to Revelation. However, the person may not have the Word in him or her.

Some people just want to be seen as distinguished. Knowing this fact, Paul wrote a letter to the Corinthians to warn them because they had gotten off track from what he had taught them, which was not to be puffed up. He taught them to be followers of him as he followed Christ. Therefore, Paul sent Timothy to bring the Corinthians into remembrance of the way Paul had led them to be Christ-like.

Apostle Paul used to be Saul of Tarsus before the power of God changed him on the road to Damascus. Saul persecuted Christians, thinking that he was doing the work of the Lord. While on the road to Damascus, he met Jesus. When Saul met Jesus, his life and name were changed. Jesus asked him in Acts 22:7b, *"Saul, Saul, why persecutest thou me?"* Saul said in Acts 22:8a, *"Who art thou, Lord?"* Saul continued by saying in Acts 22: 10a, *"What shall I do, Lord?"* Jesus told him to go to Damascus, and it would be told to him all the things appointed for him to do. There was light that shined from heaven and blinded Saul, so the men with him led him to Ananias house, a devout man of the Jews. Jesus had already spoken with Ananias that Saul was going to come to his house. Ananias told Jesus how

Saul persecuted the saints, and the chief priests had also given him authority to bind all people that called on his name. That did not phase Jesus one bit. He told Ananias to go on to his house. Saul is a chosen vessel unto him and shall bear his name before the gentle, kings and the children of Israel and how he must suffer for Him. Saul made it to Ananias house. Ananias stood before Saul and told him to receive his sight. Praise God he did; it was as if scales had fallen off of his eyes. The devil will try to keep us blind to the fact that he's trying to destroy us any way he can and end up where he is going. He knows that his destination is to be toss into the lake of fire to burn throughout eternity. Let's keep our eyes on the prize that is Jesus Christ and follow His leading.

Now, if God can use me to do street ministry in unsafe places, and if He can use Paul, a changed man, he wrote possible thirteen books of the Bible, went on missionary journeys, taught the Word of God, people threw rocks and stoned him. To top it all off, he went to prison for the work of the Lord; what about you? Allow God to use you in His Ministry.

CHAPTER 10

Meeting Kenneth and Ministering behind Prison Walls

*W*e were on the move for Jesus in the street ministry for several years, seeing people giving their lives to Jesus. That was, and still is, such a joy to me. During that season of my life, I was introduced to my husband, Kenneth Lowe, who joined us in our street ministry. We were thankful to God to have Kenneth with us, and it brought him joy to be doing the work of the Lord.

The way Kenneth and I met was quite interesting and unexpected. We met in 1989 through mutual friends, Brother Ray Clark and his wife, Pastor Sheilar Clark. They wanted to introduce me to a good brother in Christ. I told them that I was doing fine and did not want to meet anyone. They were persistent, so one day they asked me to go with them to a special meeting at Agape Church because a special guest speaker, John Avanzini, would be there.

John Avanzini was a well-known preacher who ministered on finances. I went with them. Brother Ray made sure that his wife and I were seated, then he told us he would be right back. When he came back, he had this tall, dark, muscular young man with him. When Brother Ray introduced us, the young man smiled and said that I looked just like my brother. He said that a couple of times. I was thinking, "Who is this that knows my brother?" As if he were reading my mind, he responded by telling me that he had previously met my brother.

Two weeks after meeting Kenneth, I was on my way to church one Sunday morning. I stopped at a 7-Eleven convenience store to purchase gas. While I was standing there with my son who was pumping gas, Kenneth walked by me, staring and smiling as he went into the store. I was wondering what was wrong with him. He came out of the store, still smiling, and reminded me that Brother Ray had introduced us. He began to tell me that he attended prayer meetings on Monday nights. He wanted to know if I had any prayer requests and if he could have my phone number to call me on Monday to get my prayer requests.

I was thoroughly impressed. "This man goes to prayer meetings!" I said to myself, and was led to give him my phone number. He called me the next day as he said he would do. He was on his way to prayer meeting and wanted to know, again, if I had any prayer requests. I gave him my requests, all concerning the homeless. My desire was that the homeless would have a place to live and that I could get a van to pick them up and take them to shelters. Every day after that first call, Kenneth called me.

During one of his calls, he told me that he had recently seen my brother, who had asked him if he was preaching about Jesus on the streets. Kenneth told my brother that he and another church member had passed out pamphlets about Jesus once at the Riverfest, a large annual festival on the Arkansas River in Little Rock. My brother told him that his sister, meaning me, was involved in preaching on the streets. Kenneth told him that he would like to meet me.

This conversation occurred before Brother Ray introduced me to Kenneth. It is amazing how this conversation preceded my actual introduction to Kenneth by Brother Ray. Kenneth had no idea that the "sister" that he wanted to meet would be the one who Brother Ray would later introduce him to. That is really something, how our meeting came about. That was over thirty years ago, and we have been making history together ever since.

When we were dating, one particular time, Kenneth came to visit me. He had gotten the gas bill that was lying on my desk and paid it without me knowing. Since I was unaware that the bill had been paid, I called the gas company to arrange to pay the bill. The representative told me that it was already paid in full and that I did not owe anything. I was so happy, feeling that God had canceled my debt.

Later, Kenneth and I were at a church service one Sunday night in Jacksonville, Arkansas, before getting married. I was testifying about God's goodness and the blessing of Him canceling my gas bill. After we had gotten married, Kenneth later told me that God used him to pay the bill. I asked him why he had not told me earlier, and I told him that he had me thinking that God had wiped away the debt. He said that God had wipe away the debt through him.

Kenneth is just that type of good-hearted person. It is a blessing for us to be in agreement while making out the budget, giving our tithes, and offering and helping others. We thank God for being able to pay our bills on time. Now we went through a few unpleasant changes before we got to that point.

We became members of the Full Counsel Christian Fellowship in the Spring of 1990, and we were also married during that time of the year. We went out with our street ministry a few times in 1990 before becoming involved in the ministries at our church. One day Kenneth talked with Brother Roosevelt Wilson, who was the leader of the outreach ministry at Full Counsel. Kenneth asked him if the church had a prison ministry. Brother Wilson said no, but that Kenneth could start one. Kenneth was not expecting that answer, but this is how the prison ministry began.

Brother Wilson arranged for us to go to training to become Certified Religious Assistants (CRA). Everything that we did concerning the ministry was through the approval of Pastor Silas Johnson. We went through our official training at the Pine Bluff Department of Correction. In the summer of 1990, we went to our first prison to minister as a team. When we got off the church bus at Tucker Prison, we were welcomed by a swarm of large mosquitoes, hitting us in our faces and flying all around us. I called it the initiation of the prison ministry.

Brother Wilson ministered that night, and some of the inmates came down for prayer. It was a powerful service. We were so excited, but after we got on the bus that night, we met head-on with a challenge. The bus would not start. One of the men who went with us just so happened to be a mechanic. While waiting for the bus to be repaired, we were again attacked by swarms of large mosquitoes. They had us dancing around to keep them off us, which worked to a certain extent. When the bus started, we all started thanking and praising God.

Kenneth and I were appointed as the leaders of the prison ministry at our church. Kenneth called the prisons to set up dates six months in advance for us to minister twice a month. We partnered with such Arkansas prisons as Tucker Unit, Tucker Maximum Security, Delta Regional Unit, Grimes Unit, Cummins Unit, McPherson Unit, Ouachita River Unit, Varner Unit, Wrightsville Unit, Randall L. Williams Correctional Center, Pine Bluff Women's Unit, Central Arkansas Community Correction Center, and Southeast Arkansas Community Correction Center. Our services were basically the same at each prison, and God was present at our visits.

Sometimes we had several team members with us, and at other times, only two would accompany us. Either way, we ministered with great expectations. We always encouraged the inmates to participate in the services, and they cooperated by singing and some-times giving testimonies after the Word of God went forward. We gave them an opportunity to come down for prayer and to receive Jesus as their Lord and Savior. The Bible says in Matthew 25:36b, *"I was in prison, and ye came unto me."* Therefore, it was by God's grace that we were able to go visit those that were incarcerated and share the Word of God with them.

We were also a part of the witnessing team with our church during this time. One Saturday, the witnessing team was divided into groups of two to go to a certain area of town. On that day, we were in the home of a lady to whom we were witnessing. Roaches were crawling everywhere, but we remained calm.

After the young lady offered us a seat, we sat on the sofa facing her and began telling her about the good news of Jesus Christ. We asked her if she would like to receive Jesus. She was not ready, so I asked her if we could pray for her. She said yes, and we prayed. The entire time that we were there, I looked straight at her and I did not allow the roaches to cause me to cringe.

We had been taught in our training not to be surprised and not to allow our thoughts to show on our faces or in our body language. We truly had to have self-discipline as we witnessed and ministered. The Bible says in Luke 14:23, *"And the lord said unto the servants, Go out into the highways and hedges, and compel them to come in, that my house may be filled."* Acts 1:8

says, *"But ye shall receive power, after that the Holy Ghost is come upon you: and ye shall be witnesses unto me both in Jerusalem, and in all Judaea, and in Samaria, and unto the uttermost part of the earth."* Proverbs 11:30 says, *"The fruit of the righteous is a tree of life; and he that winneth souls is wise."* We must remember that places where we witness may not be the best or most convenient. We must be willing to go because God wants us to go, and we are doing this as unto the Lord.

Now getting back to the prison ministry, another part of it is the CRA, in which we were involved. This aspect of our ministry required us to go to various barracks in the prison to minister, one-on-one, to inmates. We always went in pairs: The women went to the women's unit, and the men went to the men's unit.

I first went to the prison as a CRA with Evangelist Ernestine Thomas, who gave me on-the-job training at the Pine Bluff Women's Unit. I watched how she started the conversations and how she referred to scriptures when she answered questions the ladies had. She listened carefully to them, and afterward we prayed with them. We stayed at the unit for approximately four hours during that first visit, and I had an opportunity to minister to a few of the women. The women said that we were such a blessing to them, and I told them that they had been a blessing to us as well. It was such a joy.

The next time I went to the Pine Bluff Women's Unit was with Mother Gans. She and I took turns driving whenever we went together. In 1993, the women were moved to the Tucker Unit, which used to be a men's unit. They were there until 1998 until the McPherson Women's Unit was opened. There was also a men's unit built right across from the women's unit. The name of that unit is Grimes. They are located in Newport, Arkansas, which is about one and a half hours from Little Rock.

Throughout the years, Mother Gans and I made these trips to Newport and built a great relationship with Chaplain Harris and the women inmates. They developed an expectancy to see us. We thanked God for giving us the strength and wisdom to have Bible study, and to listen and pray for them.

The Bible says in Isaiah 50:4, "*The Lord God hath given me the tongue of the learned, that I should know how to speak a word in season to him that is weary: he wakeneth morning by morning, he wakeneth mine ear to hear as the learned.*" There were ladies that were weary, and God would give Mother Gans and I words of encouragement to speak to them. We led many of the women to the Lord and witnessed several of them released from prison and hired working in the community.

However, some women were released, but in a few months, they were back in prison. We did not condemn them. We let them know that Jesus still loved them and that He is a God of a second, third, and fourth chance. We wanted them to understand that He would give them as many chances as they needed.

Now God does not want us to keep making the same mistakes. Every day we must develop a lifestyle of reading, studying, meditating, and applying the Word of God. Doing these things, along with praying and fellowshipping with God, helps us to become stronger. We will then be as Ephesians 6:10 tells us, *"Finally, my brethren, be strong in the Lord, and in the power of his might."* We must keep God and His Word first in our lives in order to be strong.

In the late 1990s, Chaplain Mary Harris and I went to Montego Bay, Jamaica, to minister. She had connections there with a very hospitable family that took us to different areas of Montego Bay. While we were riding with our host, he was going to fast around curves and cliffs. I was holding on for dear life. I asked him to slow down and told him that I did not come there to get killed.

After that talk with him, we did not have any more issues concerning his driving. We also visited a few churches, which were great. We visited a prison in Kingston, which was called Gun Court. What a strange name for a prison. The American prisons are like condominiums compared to the prisons in Kingston. Chaplain Harris and I were glad to be used by God to encourage those that were incarcerated.

Another place that we visited was a girls' home. This home was somewhat like an orphanage. The girls all seemed so happy to see us, and we had a wonderful time with them. We took pictures with them and listened to what they had to say. Then we explained to them that Jesus loved them, and that we did, too. Chaplain Harris had brought a variety of personal hygiene products for them, and they were thankful to receive them. It was a joy to be in Jamaica spreading the gospel of Jesus Christ and witnessing in the streets, in the prison, in the nursing home, and in the girls' home.

The Bible says in *Proverbs 19:17, "He that hath pity upon the poor lendeth unto the Lord; and that which he hath given will he pay him again." Proverbs 28:27 says, "He that giveth unto the poor shall not lack: but he that hideth his eyes shall have many a curse." James 1:27 says, "Pure religion and undefiled before God and the Father is this, To visit the fatherless and widows in their affliction, and to keep himself unspotted from the world.*" We must continue to help the poor with whatever they need for day-to-day living, but most of all, we must share the Word of God with them. The Word of God can teach them how to live upright and acquire the benefits that God has for them.

The second time I went to Jamaica was in the 2000s with a group of ladies from our church and other churches supporting Pastor Jennifer Johnson. She was one of the speakers at a women's conference; God really used her. The place of worship had sidewalls like a tent. The sides walls were rolled down because it was raining, but the rain did not stop the service. I saw a lizard on top of the wall near me. As I watched the lizard, I had already made up my mind that I would get rid of him if he were to jump in my hair or on me. Thanks be to God that the lizard left. Even with this distraction, we had a powerful service.

We stayed in Jamaica for about five days. Each morning I would walk back and forth on the boat dock, praying and watching the sunrise. When it was time to leave Jamaica, there was a forecast of a hurricane. We began to pray, and we were able to leave on time because the storm went another way. I do not remember all the details, but I know that God was our protector that day!

Now, if God can use me in the prison ministry, and if He can use Pastor Jennifer Johnson and Chaplain St. Mary Harris to preach in Jamaica, what about you?

CHAPTER 11

God Uses Individuals to Aid Their Fellow Men and Women

*O*nce my husband and I were at Brown's Country Kitchen Buffet when a young man came to our table and said, "You are a preacher, aren't you?" I said yes, and he went on to say that he used to be incarcerated and that he remembered me preaching. He explained how the message really blessed him. It is always encouraging to hear that I have blessed someone. If my husband and I had been out of the will of God, we could have caused this man's faith to stumble. He probably would not have come over to our table, and he probably would have been surprised to see us acting contrary to God's Word.

Our behavior can help or hinder, and we do not always know who is following our example. The Bible says that we are living epistles being read by many. We are to live a lifestyle pleasing to God, walking in love, kindness, and true holiness. The question is, "What are people reading when they see us?" Do not get me wrong; we all make mistakes. When we do, we should repent and continue to grow in the Lord.

I must admit, in the earlier years of our marriage, Kenneth and I had a few heated discussions at times. The discussion got so hot that I packed my son's and my clothes and went to my mother's house. We stayed for almost a week. I remember calling Pastor Silas, telling him certain things about Kenneth, and I felt I was right. I told our pastor that I had left Kenneth. Pastor Silas told me to go back home because Kenneth needed me. Looking back over the years, I realize that I needed him just as much as he needed me. We complement each other. I am thankful that I went back; Kenneth is thankful, also. However, I did not want to hear what Pastor Silas had to say about the situation at that time, but I am so glad that I listened to him.

Kenneth and I led the prison ministry for thirteen years, seeing hundreds of men and women give their lives to the Lord. During that time, Kenneth set up a meeting with our Pastor to ask a question concerning the ministry. Before the meeting, we had already made peace with whatever the answer would be. If the Pastor were to say no to our request, we would not be offended.

When we met with Pastor Silas, Kenneth asked him if he would sponsor him through the church to be a missionary chaplain at the Wrightsville Unit. Pastor Silas did not bat an eye, nor did he clear his throat; he said yes and did not ask Kenneth any questions before he gave that answer.

Afterward, Pastor Silas asked Kenneth how much he was making on his job. Kenneth told him, and Pastor said that he would give Kenneth the same salary. My husband gratefully took on this new position as the church's missionary chaplain. We were so thankful. Kenneth was a missionary chaplain at the Wrightsville Unit sent out from Full Counsel Christian Fellowship Church for almost two years. At that time, there were not many men of color in that position of missionary chaplain in Arkansas. Kenneth helped Chaplain Guy a great deal once he learned what to do. The inmates were blessed as well.

In 2001, Kenneth was hired as a Field Director with the Chuck Colson Prison Ministries. His job was to contact churches and ministries in Arkansas coordinate teams to go inside the prisons to minister to the men and women, even though there were already churches involved in ministering to the inmates. Each year the ministry operated the Angel Tree Project throughout the state. They contacted ministries and churches to participate in getting Christmas gifts for children whose parents were incarcerated. It was such a blessing to so many families.

Kenneth also helped organize an annual event called Operations Starting Line, where the Word of God went forward. The ministry team encouraged and prayed for the inmates and passed out informational brochures. Thank God for the souls saved and the encouraging word during these meetings, along with a Christian Band and testimonies. This event took place outside on the prison grounds whenever the weather was clear. The excitement was in the atmosphere; you could see it on the men and women faces.

Even though Kenneth and I were highly involved in ministry, we made sure that we spent quality time with our family. Some of this quality time included my mother. She would sometimes be with us, enjoying her older years of life. I am so thankful that I was able to be there for her as she became older. If I had been still bounded by the devil, I would not have had a mind to help take care of my mother. The Lord allowed me to be a positive witness to my entire family. Kenneth and I give God all the glory and praise for using us in such a powerful way. As we worked with the Lord in His ministry, we also grew in Him, displaying His attributes where others could see His good works in us and glorify our heavenly Father.

The Bible says in Acts 16:16–40 that Paul and Silas were thrown into jail because Paul cast a spirit of divination out of a young girl who brought her masters much gain. The young slave girl had followed Paul and Silas around for several days. As she followed them, she repeatedly used her mocking spirit of divination to say that Paul and Silas were the servants of the Most High God. What she was saying was true, but it was with the wrong spirit. Paul was grieved, so he cast the foul spirit out of the young slave girl and set her free. We need to know by the Spirit of God who is speaking into our lives.

The damsel's masters were upset because they no longer profit from the damsel since Paul had commanded the spirit of divination (soothsaying, fortune-telling) to come out of her. Therefore, these men accused Paul and Silas of troubling the city and teaching unlawful things for the city. These men proceeded to have Paul and Silas stripped and thrown in jail.

Nowadays, in the United States, people do not go to jail for teaching false doctrines. Many philosophers, theologians, pastors, and ministers would be in prison if that were the case. However, a person can go to prison for a long time for false accusations of a crime. Some of these people are later found to be innocent. When we become Christians, we must not think that we are immune from persecution or being falsely accused. If we keep the connection with our Lord and Savior Jesus Christ, staying in the Word and living the Word, we will have the peace of God that surpasses all understanding and trusting Him.

This is exactly what Paul and Silas did when they were falsely accused, so they are our examples.

Paul and Silas had a personal relationship with the Lord; they began to pray and sing praises unto God at midnight. Suddenly, there was an earthquake. The jailhouse doors opened, and the shackles were loose from all the prisoners, but everyone remained in their cells. Many of you know this story.

The jailer saw the opened doors and immediately thought that the prisoners had escaped because he had been sleeping. The jailer thought that he was in trouble and prepared to kill himself with the sword.

Paul told the jailer not to harm himself because the prisoners were all still there. Since the prisoners were led to remain in the cells and not attempt to escape, the jailer's heart was touched so much that he wanted to know what he must do to be saved. Paul told him to believe in the Lord Jesus; he did, and so was the jailer's family were saved. That night sleeping on the job paid off for the jailer. These scriptures in Acts 16:16–40 are so profound.

Now, if God can use Pastor Silas Johnson to give me sound counseling when I was about to walk away from my marriage, and if God can use Pastor Silas to allow Kenneth to be sent out to the prison as a Missionary Chaplain, and if God can use Paul and Silas to stand up for righteousness, being a positive example in jail, what about you?

CHAPTER 12

The Gift

*I*n 1992, I was sitting in a New Year's Eve service. Pastor Silas said that in 1993 God was going to use Pastor Jennifer, his wife, to pull gifts out of people. So, I sat there wondering, "What's on the inside of me that she can pull out, that I have no idea is there?" I could not think of one thing.

The following year, Pastor Jennifer asked me to write a skit for our upcoming women's retreat. I said that I would, even though I had never written a skit before. I also told her that I would pray and ask God to show me what to write and to help me. She told me the skit title, "Get Real," and the characters' names. When I presented the finished skit to her, she said it was just what she wanted. That is how I started writing skits and plays. I never liked writing letters before, so it had to be God who enabled me to write skits and plays and now this book.

God placed me at the right place at the right time that New Year's Eve night because He had a word for me through my Pastors. Pastor Jennifer had mentioned that she started to ask someone else to help me write the skit, but she said, "God said, no, Sister Lowe."

My first skit, "Get Real," was initially performed at Pastor Jennifer Johnson's A Call To Excellence Ministries (ACTE) Spring Conference, held in Hot Springs, Arkansas. One of the speaker's was Minister Gardener from San Antonio, Texas. She was impressed how much the skit ministered to everyone, so at her next meeting in Texas, her group of ladies acted out the skit. I was so surprised and happy.

Since I was present at the performance, Minister Gardener asked me to stand. She introduced me and made encouraging remarks to me. The audience gave me a round of applause, and I give God all the praise and glory for using me. "Get Real" was also performed at the McPherson Women's Prison in Newport, Arkansas. The women at the prison were very tuned in to the skit and appreciative that we would take the time to present it to them.

Another thing that Pastor Jennifer asked me years ago is if I would get a group of women together and pray for the ACTE Conferences before the start dates and I did. There were times we had all-night prayer meetings, which were such a blessing to our ministry. At times I would arrive a day before the conferences to set the atmosphere by praying in the conference room where the meeting was going to take place. God moved mightily in those meetings. I'm so honored to have been a part of the ACTE Ministries.

We saw people delivered, saved, and healed. We also witnessed blinded eyes opened, and we left empowered with the Holy Ghost. Hallelujah! I thank God for Sister Valerie Waites, a mighty woman of God, always praying for ACTE. She helped me tremendously by taking care of the monthly calendar and scheduling people to pray and fast for the ministry. Sister Valerie still handles that task today. She was, and still is, a true blessing to me and others.

While I was working on my second production, which was a dramatic live stage play entitled "The Prodigal Daughter," God spoke to my spirit. He said that the writing gift had been lying dormant within me but had now been released. I just broke down in tears. At that moment, I remembered how I really enjoyed my speech and drama classes in high school. I now know why I liked those classes so much. This gift was in me all along, but I did not realize it was there. I never thought that I would be writing, directing, and producing live stage play productions, doing something positive with my life.

If you do not already know what special gift or gifts you have from God or do not know your purpose in this life, ask God, your heavenly Father. He will let you know. If He does not let you know in a few days, keep expecting your answer, even if it takes a few years or longer.

In the meantime, whatsoever Jesus tells you to do, do it. This reference comes from John 2:5 *"His mother saith unto the servants, whatsoever he saith unto you, do it."* Ecclesiastes 9:10 says, *"Whatsoever thy hand findeth to do, do it with thy might; for there is no work, nor device, nor knowledge, nor wisdom, in the grave, whither thou goest."*

Please do not take your gifts and talent to the grave when you die but use them here on earth to be a blessing to others. Brothers, if you know that your neighbor is ill and not able to mow his or her lawn, mow it for them or pay someone to take care of it. That is putting your hands to good work. At church, find out where you can help. Furthermore, if there is something you can do at your child's school, become a volunteer. Colossians 3:23 says, *"And whatsoever ye do, do it heartily, as to the Lord, and not unto men;"*

In the gospels, when Jesus called His disciples to follow Him, they were working. For instance, Peter and his brother Andrew were casting their nets, and they left the nets to follow Jesus. James and John were mending their nets on their father's boats, but when Jesus called them, they dropped their nets to follow Him.

Please do not waste your time sitting on your sofa eating ice cream and cookies and waiting on God. Some of you know your gifts and callings but do not want to walk in them because they may not be as glamorous as someone else's. The Bible says that it is not wise to compare ourselves with others. Be thankful that God has blessed you with a gift and walk in it because someone is waiting for what you have to offer them. You will be blessed by sharing your gift. I know that I am blessed when I share my gift with others. It would be best if you did not take unused gifts to the grave with you. Instead, obey God and walk in your calling.

By the grace of God, I have written several skits and plays. It amazes me to see how God uses me in such a way to inspire and encourage others, giving them joy, hope, and laughter. We have also seen people give their lives to the Lord after seeing the different situations reenacted in the plays. The productions helped viewers understand some of their own concerns. For instance, we saw this happen when we performed "The Devil's

Supper," which I wrote in 1995 and still just as powerful in all of the productions through the years. The play openly revealed the tricks and craftiness of the devil. In the play, the devil called fifteen of his demons to a supper. The table is set with real food, such as green bean casserole, turkey legs, fried chicken, angel eggs (deviled eggs), cornbread, rolls, pies, cakes, and drinks.

The devil called in the spirits of lies, fornication, hatred, murder, and many other evil spirits. The spirits were all dressed in formal clothing, looking good. The devil gave them all after-dinner orders to go attack various individuals and families. In the particular family portrayed in the play, the husband had a job making a large six-figure salary. The family lived in a beautiful home, and the couple had everything they wanted. Their daughter was in a prestigious private school. However, all of this changed when the husband's job had a tremendous decline in business. One evening he prepared dinner for the family.

As they sat down to eat, his wife began explaining, in a high-pitched voice, how her day had gone. She then asked her daughter how her day had progressed. The daughter explained that her day had been horrible because the other students had made fun of her, saying that her family was not rich anymore. As the scene developed, the spirit of murder continuously walked around the family, waving his hands over their heads, and making gestures of murder. Of course, the family could not see this spirit of murder. The spirit was visible to the audience only.

The father encouraged his wife and daughter to eat and enjoy their meal. At that moment, the daughter started coughing and said, "Mama, I can't breathe." As the mother leaned over to her daughter, she said, "Honey, what have you done?" The daughter then collapsed and died. All of the issues with the family's finances had caused the father to feel that the problems were his fault since he could not provide for his family in his usual manner. He said that he could not take it anymore. The result was that he had poisoned his family and himself. Therefore, they all perished.

After the performances of this production, one of the cast members informed me that a young lady told her that her husband had committed suicide a couple of years ago. Seeing this play gave her closure concerning the death of her husband because it helped her to understand how he must have been struggling with the storms of life. She was so glad that she had come to the production. The plays that God has blessed me to write are thought-provoking and encouraging. Many of them give answers to questions that the viewers may have had for quite some time because of the real-life situations that are portrayed.

I wrote another play titled "When a Man Loves a Woman." This play is based on the book of Hosca, who was one of the minor prophets in the Bible. I adapted my play to modern times. It is about a man named Sonny, who loved his wife, Kisha, so much. Even when he found out about her having affairs with other men, he forgave her time after time. Even so, he began to doubt if their three children were really his. Therefore, he had a DNA test done and found out that he was the father of only one of the children. He was so hurt, but he still treated them all the same. Moreover, Sonny did not let his wife know that he knew about the children until near the end of the play.

One of his wife's lovers, Carlos, followed her home one day because he loved her so much and wanted to ask her to marry him. He had no idea that she was already married. Carlos knocked on the door, and Sonny answered, Carlos stepped inside and asked if Kisha was there, not knowing that Sonny was Kisha's husband. Sonny asked Carlos, "Who are you?" Carlos replied, "The question is, who are you?" Carlos continued. "I get it. You are Kisha's brother."

Speechless, Sonny did not respond, so Carlos went on to say that he wanted to marry Kisha. Carlos then said to Sonny, "and you can be my best man," still assuming that Sonny was Kisha's brother.

As the play goes on, the two fellows fight, and Sonny throws Carlos out of the house. In this play, the wife asked her husband to forgive her again. She saw the light and was serious this time. Her husband forgave her, and she changed her ways for good by asking Jesus to come into her life. The redemptive power and love of God are displayed in this production.

God does not tell us everything that we will do with our gifts and talents at the beginning. We truly must trust God and follow His leading. Isaiah 1:19 says, *"If ye be willing and obedient, ye shall eat the good of the land."* We must be willing not grudgingly but ready to obey God, trusting Him, and we will have a fulfilling life journey.

Therefore, if we want to please God, we must trust Him regardless of what the situation looks like or sounds like in the physical realm. Psalms 37:23 says, *"The steps of a good man are ordered by the Lord: and he delighteth in his way."* We must allow the Lord Jesus to order our steps, and where the Lord leads us, we will follow. If God can use my Pastors to speak into my life and if God can use me to write powerful plays of His redemption and His saving grace, what about you?

CHAPTER 13

God's Blessings through Others

*R*eading a script and hearing a script read aloud stirs interest and causes curiosity to arise. The same sensibility happens when you see it unfold right before your very eye. The cast takes the script to another level when it comes off the pages to life on stage. The facial expressions, the body language, and certainly spoken words convey a message that touches the heart. The viewers get so involved that they talk to the characters as if they are acquainted with them. I love hearing and seeing the audience's reactions. God has blessed me with so many wonderful gifted and talented people who have helped me give our drama ministry divine purpose.

Our cast members are such a blessing to us and to everyone who sees them in character. We have a changeover in some cast members every couple of years, with some remaining with the ministry much longer. This change is understandable, especially since they serve on a volunteer basis. They do an outstanding job as they serve God in the process.

Even though we do bless the cast and crew with a stipend at times, there will be a day when we will pay everyone their pay scale with incentives. I can honestly say that they are doing it as unto the Lord.

We rehearse three to four months before the performances, rehearsing twice a week, and two weeks before the performance, we rehearse three to four times a week. Sometimes the last night of rehearsal does not look too promising, but the day or night of the production is always as smooth as clockwork. God continues to give the increase.

The many individuals God placed in my life to assist me in the drama ministry have shared so much of their time and talent and are still sharing. I could not have accomplished any of the productions by myself. There is one brother that Kenneth and I have known for years; his name is Brother Bernard Randle. We met in the 1980s at a church that we used to attend, Faith Temple Missionary Baptist Church. We both helped with the Children's Church Ministry. The director of the Children's Church asked us to find and purchase a few puppets for the children, so we did. The puppets were such a hit with the children that the pastor asked us to do a short puppet show for the congregation one Sunday morning. The members were so impressed; it brought so much laughter and joy to the church.

Two years later, Brother Randle and I served together in the drama department at another church, Full Counsel Christian Fellowship. I received many years of on-the-job training and eventually became one of the drama department leaders. Brother Randle has faithfully assisted me as the assistant director and stage manager in our drama ministry, Lifting Up Jesus Christ Ministries (LUJCM).

In the ministry my husband and I started, Brother Randle was the leading character in one of the early performances then and even now. The roles that he plays are a perfect fit for him. From the day he began working with us, Brother Randle often arrives at rehearsals early, setting up the scenes with the props. He takes his role as a stage manager very seriously, taking ownership and pride in his operational role.

Brother Randle uses the list of items we need for each scene to visualize where the furniture and accessories should be placed. He usually has a few men lined up on the day or night of the production, assisting with putting the furniture in the progressive order of the scenes. We have worked together to demonstrate to the cast how they should portray each character. Brother Randle always informs the cast and me when he makes adjustments to the scripts. However, he respectfully says, "Sister Lowe has the final say." Kenneth and I are so thankful for Brother Randle being a part of the ministry and sharing his wisdom with us.

When it came to having props made for the church, we attended at that time and our ministry productions. I called on another faithful servant of the Lord, Brother Elijah Hill. He is a master of carpentry. I had only to describe what I wanted to be built, and he could make it with such expertise. For instance, I wanted two carriages designed to be carried by four men each. The carriages were to have rods on which curtains were to be hung. They turned out perfectly. He made two sets of roller curtains for changing of the scenes and portable stages.

Furthermore, he constructed tall and short columns that brought more beauty to the stage. Brother Hill came and helped put props together and take them apart. His wife, Sister Shirley Hill, designed the portable curtains and the skirts for the portable platforms. She currently has us on her prayer list, and we are so thankful for her and her husband always ready to help in any way that they can.

The Hills have a son named Shaun. Ever since he was a teenager, he has helped in the sound department at church, and he still does many years later. In his early years of working in the church, he realized that I needed a pair of walkie-talkies, and he bought me a pair. They were yellow, my favorite color. God is so good! I was surprised and thankful that he thought enough of me to get them for me. Shaun is our sound man for LUJCM. A month before the productions, he attends the rehearsals to set up the microphones on everyone in preparation for the play to do a mic and voice check. He also sits in the booth with the venue's sound tech person to make sure there are no technical issues. The Hill family is indeed a blessing to our ministry.

God blessed us with an anointed and gifted musician, Maestro Jansen Goodwin, who plays music that profoundly fits the productions. He can take the music to a high, perplexed state as the character portrays a confused person; then, he can bring the music to a mellow and calming sound that brings even more life to the plays. He not only plays scene music, also ministering music for those that minister in song. I remember once a sister said to me years ago before the maestro came on board, "Sister Lowe, you should have a musician by now." I told her that I had prayed for God to send me one that could assist me. During that time, I was using cassettes and later CDs, which were working well. Still, I wanted an anointed musician.

When I attended church functions, I would sometimes ask the musician if he or she would be interested in playing for a production. No one ever got back in touch with me, but God allowed Maestro Jansen and I to meet through a mutual friend, Pastor Kevin Riley. Maestro Jansen has been a blessing since I met him. We thank you so much Maestro Jansen by the grace of God you have taken us to another level. Zechariah 4:10a (NLT) says, *"Do not despise these small beginnings, for the Lord rejoices to see the work begin."*

Therefore, my brothers and sisters, I do not despise small beginnings; I am not disgusted by my humble beginnings of writing and producing, having to use cassette players. I thank God that I had a mind and boldness to start, not knowing how it would turn out. There is a scripture in the book of James that says that faith without works is dead. So, we took steps of faith, and our works followed. So, allow the Lord to rejoice over you to see the work begin that He has given you to do.

Sister Onessa Crumpton is another one of our vessels of God. Her voice is so crisp and clear, and she can demonstrate an amazing range from the lowest to the highest. The presence of God is vivid in her songs when she ministers, with and without music. The audience is sometimes moved to tears from her anointed praise and worship ministry, even in rehearsals.

There are times we just have to take a praise break because the anointing is so strong that it urges us to give God the praise and the glory right then. On these occasions, there is a relief in the atmosphere, a sense of peace permeates the room. Once the production is over, the songs are still ministering to our hearts and in the hearts of the audience. What a joy! Sister Onessa has been with us for several years, ministering in songs and acting. She is such a blessing to the ministry.

Brother Robert Bolden has been the leading male character in our drama ministry for several years. He is a very dedicated cast member. Sometimes he knows many of his lines after the first couple of rehearsals because he takes the appropriate time to get into character. Once after one of the productions, he and other cast members went to a restaurant. A woman who had attended the play and recognized Brother Bolden, who had played the character Sonny, a loving and kind husband.

The woman said, "I wish that I had a man like Sonny." She said it loud enough for Brother Bolden to hear her, and he looked at her and smiled. This is just one example of how his acting impacts the audience. I give God the praise for sending Brother Bolden our way. These plays have great value and meaning, and they leave the audience emotionally intrigued and blessed.

Sister Marion Smith was the leading lady in many of our plays for several years until she moved to another state. The way that she became involved is very interesting. One day after church, I told her that the Lord had shown me in a dream that she would be in the play that I was preparing for production. Sister Marion laughed and said, "He didn't show you me." I gave her a script and asked if she would come to one of the rehearsals. She did come, and the rest is history. Praise God!

In one of the plays, she played a teenager by the name of Stephanie. Her father was a pastor, so she was raised in a Christian home. Stephanie was a rebellious and outspoken child. As the play develops, she ended up serving time in prison, where, as an adult, she rededicated her life back to Jesus. Afterward, she went to college and became a counselor for children. She helped them get on the right path, using her knowledge from firsthand experience. Stephanie related to the children in a way that expressed her understanding of what they were experiencing.

Years later, while Sister Marion was at a Kroger grocery store, she heard someone call her Stephanie. She kept on walking, so the woman grasped Marion's arm and turned her around. She said, "I am upset with you for making all those wrong decisions." Marion told the woman that it was a play and that her name was Marion. The woman replied that she would always be Stephanie to her and said, "Your parents didn't raise you that way." Sister Marion told the woman that Stephanie rededicated her life to the Lord. However, the woman did not want to hear that. This situation shows that live stage plays, and movies can greatly impact the viewers, even for years to come. However, some viewers focus on a particular scene and miss the overall meaning, as the woman in Kroger did. The good thing is that she still took away some good points from the play.

When I was in the world, not knowing Jesus Christ as my Lord and Savior, I had an acquaintance named Brenda Johnson. We used to work at a liquor warehouse together and had our own liquor store in the trunk of our cars and purses, if you know what I mean. It was cash and carry, which worked well for us until the company moved. They did not hire us back at their new location.

It is so ironic that Brenda and I both were saved on separate occasions and later became members of the same church. This was a surprise to both of us. We were even in the drama department together. Brenda Johnson has a unique gift of making people laugh. She brings so much joy and laughter to the character roles, and she also does that in her everyday life. I appreciate Brenda so much for bringing her humor to us when we need it the most.

Chris Rudley is another person who God allowed to cross my path. Chris was about fourteen years old when I met him. He was very well mannered and was doing an outstanding job as a member of the dance troop at church. I have watched him over the years grow into a strong Christian man. Whatever he put his hands to do, he did it with enthusiasm, and acting is a God-given talent for him. He also sometimes assisted Brother Randle and me with coaching cast members.

For many years, Chris assisted us with our LUJCM live production stage plays. He took on the responsibility of welcoming the audience and praying for those who needed prayer. God is blessing him in ministering to youth and adults today, and he is also a Christian comedian with a good sense of humor. He has been a tremendous asset to the ministry.

I have had an opportunity to teach drama to many children who have been a part of our drama ministry, ranging from age five years old to 18 teenagers. They were excited about being a part of the drama ministry and showing their talents to their parents and the church. I have seen many of them grow up and have productive lives and have children of their own. I thank God for Bishop Silas and Dr. Jennifer Johnson for allowing me to serve and work with the children in the drama ministry. This experience sharpened my skills and allowed me to use the gift that God gave me and continue to bring joy and laughter to others.

We still have children involved in the productions, sharing their acting gifts, tap dancing, and praise dancing. It is such a joy to see the excitement and enthusiasm in their eyes as they display their gifts and talents.

God will call people alongside you to help bring to pass the vision, the assignment, and the dream He has given you. We are blessed to be a blessing to others. Genesis 12:2 says, *"And I will make of thee a great nation, and I will bless thee, and make thy name great; and thou shalt be a blessing."*

There was a time when I needed a place to have rehearsals, so I asked a pastor, who was a realtor if he knew any reasonably priced places that I could rent. He told me that I could rehearse at his church for no charge. I was so thankful. Pastor Kevin Riley gave me a key and the alarm system codes to his church. Now, as anyone can see, that was the favor of God. We rehearsed at his church for approximately two years, and he also very convincingly performed in one of our productions many years ago. Pastor Kevin Riley has truly been a blessing to our ministry, and I thank God for his heart of compassion.

There is another person, Felicia Anderson, who has helped me tremendously. She has a gift of graphic design, one of the ways she uses her gift is to design our flyers and programs. When she finishes with them, they are top-of-the-line in creativity. She takes the pictures of characters that I want on the flyers and creates a remarkable background design. Sometimes I describe to her how I want the flyers to look, and she accomplishes that task, going above and beyond what I asked. Even when I do not have any ideas, she does. I Thank God for Sister Felicia Anderson; she is such a blessing to the body of Christ.

Moreover, Evangelist Faye Mosby Long has genuinely been a blessing to our entire drama ministry with her friendship for over twenty years. Even though we do not talk to each other that often, there is such a kindred spirit between us. She has blessed the ministry by making DVD commercials, which feature cast members, on Facebook. Evangelist Faye always does a professional job, and many years ago, she was in one of our productions. She played the spirit of gluttony in a very realistic way. Evangelist Faye is also a recording artist who has sung at several of our productions. I am so thankful to know her.

Another person who has worked with me is Minister Veronica Ayers, the general manager of KJBN AM radio station. She has created such intriguing radio advertisements for our productions. Her commercials are so dynamic that the listeners cannot wait to see the productions. She uses a few cast clips, a little snippet of songs, and a male announcer voice, which is dramatically inviting. All of Minister Ayers commercials are outstanding. When she is working with us on commercials, we do not feel rushed or intimidated, as she generates ideas that fit perfectly with our intent. I thank God for her.

My husband, Kenneth Lowe, has been the best supporter on my journey. He prays for me, encourages me, and is a sounding board for me. In other words, I ask and say things to him to see what he thinks about them. He tells me his thoughts on the matter, and I do take some of his suggestions.

There was a time when a particular furniture store allowed us to use some of their beautiful furniture for scenes in a play. The owner allowed us to use different pieces of furniture for a few of our plays, based on what we needed for that specific production. We were very thankful for the furniture store owner allowing us to use his furniture. I was somewhat content, but Kenneth was not. He wanted us to have our own furniture for the productions. We could have charged the furniture on our credit card, but we did not want to do that. We had some extra money, but I had planned to do something else with it.

Kenneth made it clear that he did not want me to continue asking to use someone else's furniture. We were blessed with more extra money, and he said, "Let's buy furniture for the ministry," and that is what we did.

He also did the accounting for the ministry for a couple of years when our accountant died the latter part of 2017; Roy was not only our accountant, but he was also one of our dearest friends, we really miss Roy. However, God blessed us with another accountant in 2019 and I thank God for her. My husband working in the ministry with me is such a blessing in so many ways.

There are so many more people that God has allowed to be a blessing to me and my calling. All of these people have made a huge impact on the success of my gift of producing plays. I pray for all of them and others that have sown into the ministry that God has given me. I pray that they receive a hundred-fold return, and that people will come alongside them to help them carry out what God has called them to do. I also pray that the gifts that God has given them will be stirred up even more, and that they will move forward with a greater tenacity than ever before.

Now, the question is, if God can use others to be a blessing, what about you? Remember that we are called to be a blessing.

CHAPTER 14

Key Concepts to Help Fulfill Our Purpose

*I*n all our lives, unfavorable situations will arise, but we must not lose focus. We must set our face like a flint, not looking to the left or right; in other words, we must not be moved by what we see or hear. God will give us step-by-step instructions on how to accomplish what he has called us to do. Listed below are concepts that are very valuable to me. As I routinely engage in them, they are helping me to fulfill the plan and purpose that God has for me. I pray that they will be a blessing to help you as well.

1. **Prayer**: Prayer should be a daily part of our lives. We must commune with God, fellowship with Him, thank Him, praise Him, petition Him, listen to His voice, and obey.

Philippians 4:6 (ESV) *"Do not be anxious about anything, but in everything by prayer and supplication with thanksgiving let your request be made known to God."*

Jeremiah 33:3 (ESV) *"Call to me and I will answer you, and will tell you great and hidden things that you have not known."*

John 10:27 *"My sheep hear my voice, and I know them, and they follow me."*

Proverbs 3:6 *"In all thy ways acknowledge him, and he shall direct thy paths."*

2. **Faith**: We must have confidence and trust God as His Word says, desiring to please only Him. If He tells us to do something that we do not comprehend at the time, we must not try to figure it out. The key is to "just do it."

   Hebrews 11:6 *"But without faith it is impossible to please him: for he that cometh to God must believe that he is,* and that he is a rewarder of them that diligently seek him."

2 Corinthians 5: 7 *"(For we walk by faith, not by sight.)"*

James 2:17–18 17 *"Even so faith, if it hath not works, is dead, being alone."* 18 *"Yea, a man may say, Thou hast faith, and I have works: shew me thy faith without thy works, and I will shew thee my faith by my works."*

3. **Read/study/meditate/do:** The Word of God will grow us. By applying His word to our lives, we will grow in grace and faith. We must consume the word each day. In doing this, we will get wisdom, knowledge, and understanding from the Word. Changing each day more and more into the image of Jesus Christ.

> **2 Timothy 2:15** *"Study to shew thyself approved unto God, a workman that needeth not to be ashamed, rightly dividing the word of truth."*

2 Timothy 3:16–17 16 *"All scripture is given by inspiration of God, and is profitable for doctrine, for reproof, for correction, for instruction in righteousness:" 17 "That the man of God may be perfect, thoroughly furnished unto all good works."*

James 1:22a *"But be ye doers of the word, and not hearers only."*

Joshua 1:8 *"This book of the law shall not depart out of thy mouth; but thou shall meditate there in day and night, that thou mayest observe to do according to all that is written therein: for then thou shall make thy way prosperous, and then thou shalt have good success."*

4. **Vision:** God can speak directly to us about His designated purpose for us here on earth, and He also can speak to us through one of His anointed vessels. When He speaks, catch on to His words and "see" His plan. Be sure to write it down. It may take a while for the plan to come to fruition, but do not lose hope and faith. Continue to believe.

> **Habakkuk 2:2–3** 2 *"And the Lord answered me, and said, Write the vision, and make it plain upon tables, that he may run that readeth it."* 3 *"For the vision is yet for an appointed time, but at the end it shall speak, and not lie: though it tarry, wait for it; because it will surely come, it will not tarry."*

5. **Plan:** The principal aspect of attaining a vision is to plan. For example, if your vision is to start a business, you must organize and complete several tasks. Some of these tasks may include determining a name for the business, researching, and completing the paperwork needed for the business to be legitimate, determining a location, acquiring the necessary equipment, and developing a market plan. Naturally, there are several other duties that you would need to perform.

> **Luke 14:28** *"For which of you, intending to build a tower, sitteth not down first, and counteth the cost, whether he have sufficient to finish it?"*

> **Proverbs 16:3** *"Commit thy works unto the Lord, and thy thoughts shall be established."*

6. **Patience:** According to the Oxford English Dictionary, patience is "the ability to stay calm and accept a delay, or something annoying without complaining." We must allow patience to have its perfect work in us because there will be delays, hurts, and misunderstandings. Remember that our timing is not God's timing.

> **1 Corinthians 13:4** *"Love is patient, love is kind. It does not envy, it does not boast, it is not proud."*

> **Romans 12:12** *"Rejoicing in hope; patient in tribulation; continuing instant in prayer."*

> **Galatians 6:9** *"And let us not be weary in well doing: for in due season we shall reap, if we faint not."*

7. **Awareness of the Adversary:** We have an enemy wanting to destroy us. This enemy is the devil. He

does not want us to fulfill what God has called us to do. We must have discernment and fight the devil with the Word of God, just like Jesus did, we do not fight people verbally nor physically. We are not in a flesh and blood battle.

1 Peter 5:8–10 8 *"Be sober, be vigilant; because your adversary the devil, as a roaring lion, walketh about, seeking whom he may devour:"* 9 *"Whom resist steadfast in the faith, knowing that the same afflictions are accomplished in your brethren that are in the world."* 10 *"But the God of all grace, who hath called us unto his eternal glory by Christ Jesus, after that ye have suffered a while, make you perfect, stablish, strengthen, settle you."*

John 10:10 *"The thief cometh not, but for to steal, and to kill, and to destroy: I am come that they might have life, and that they might have it more abundantly."*

James 4:7–8a 7 *"Submit yourselves therefore to God. Resist the devil, and he* *will flee from you." 8a "Draw nigh to God, and he will draw nigh to you."*

2 Corinthians 10:3–6 3 *"For though we walk in the flesh, we do not war after the flesh"* 4 *"(For the weapons of our warfare are not carnal, but mighty through God to the pulling down of strong holds)"* 5 *"Casting down imaginations, and every high thing that exalteth itself against the knowledge of God, and bringing into captivity every thought to the obedience of Christ"* 6 *"And having in a readiness to revenge all disobedience, when your obedience is fulfilled."*

8. **Wait:** Wait means to stay or rest in expectation or to stay where one is and delay actions until a particular time or until something else happens. When we are working with God to fulfill our purpose, we must wait on His timing and His leading. We must not get anxious and do things the way we think they should be done. We must wait on the Lord.

Psalms 27:13–14 13 *"I had fainted, unless I had believed to see the goodness*

*of the Lord in the land of the living." 14
"Wait on the Lord: be of good courage,
and he shall strengthen thine heart: wait,
I say, on the Lord."*

9. **Temperance**: We are required to have emotional restraint and self-control. We must have these virtues in our lives in order to do what God has called us to do. We should not allow our flesh to dictate to us how we are going to react in any given situation. As children of God, we must represent Him as His Word says.

> **Philippians 4:4–5** 4 *"Rejoice in the Lord always: and again I say, rejoice."* 5 *"Let your moderation be known unto all men. The Lord is at hand."*

> **2 Peter 1:5–6** 5 *"And beside this, giving all diligence, add to your faith virtue; and to virtue knowledge;"* 6 *"And to knowledge temperance; and to temperance patience; and to patience godliness."*

> **Titus 2:11–12** 11 *"For the grace of God that bringeth salvation hath appeared to*

all men," 12 *"Teaching us that, denying ungodliness and worldly lusts, we should live soberly, righteously, and godly, in this present world."*

May you always have Jesus in your heart and on your mind. Always do things to please Him. If God can use me to incorporate these concepts in my life, what about you?

CHAPTER 15

God Will Do It!

I continue to write, direct, and conduct live productions. We were scheduled to be at the Ron
Robinson Theater, located in the River Market District
in Little Rock, Arkansas, on June 6, 2020. We post-
poned our plans because of the pandemic and the need
to social distancing.

In the latter part of March, we started rehearsing
by way of telephone to be ready for June, thinking that
the pandemic would have subsided by then. However,
when we realized that we would not perform in June,
we discontinued our rehearsals in May and will resume
in God's timing.

As founders of Lifting Up Jesus Christ Ministries
(LUJCM), our drama ministry, is a 501(c)(3) non-
profit organization. We will continue to believe
God to help us build a five-hundred-seat theater in
the Little Rock area. This theater will be where live

stage productions will bring laughter, joy, and hope to everyone who attends.

Our theater will provide jobs for the community and be a positive example for the public. We plan to also present thirty-minute matinees on Saturdays at least twice a month, at which youth will usher, perform in the stage plays, and operate the ticket counters and concession stand. The youth participation will give them a sense of responsibility as they engage in positive activities; keep in mind, they will always have adult supervision.

Furthermore, we trust God to enable the theater to be a haven for children who are going through difficult situations in their homes and schools.

It will also be a place for children who are not going through challenging conditions. Consequently, with God's help, inside the facility will be a Theatrical School of Arts (TSOA) and a Character Development Center (CDC).

Our vision is that the TSOA will offer acting, puppetry, and dance classes such as tap, creative mime, ballet, cultural dancing, and square dancing. These types will give the youth an excellent alternative and a positive outlook on life and help steer them away from involvement in drugs, alcohol, violence, bullying, illicit sex, and teen pregnancy. Their minds will be filled with positive thoughts and will not settle for the same old status quo.

The CDC will have a remarkable curriculum, being taught by loving, caring, and qualified instructors. Students will range from six to eighteen years of age. It will also include classes in etiquette, positive character development, build confidence, self-esteem, decision-making skills, emotional stability and much more.

We will equip today's youth with the knowledge of how to face and handle challenges now and when they become adults. The youth will be an asset rather than a lability to our society, making a positive difference everywhere they go. They can dream and do things beyond their imagination and their expectations because the sky will be limitless. We must remember that today's youth are the leaders of the future.

I do not know when the theater and all of its entities will come to pass. Still, I know it will be in God's timing.

My vision reminds me of Joseph's two dreams: One was about his brothers bowing down to him, and the second dream was about his father, his mother (not Rachel because she died while giving birth to Benjamin), and his eleven brothers bowing down to him. You can find this account in Genesis 37:5–10.

Joseph did not know when his dreams would come to pass; he did not know that he would go through many trials and tribulations before becoming a ruler in Egypt before those dreams would become his reality. The same is true with us. We do not know all the things that we will go through on this journey, but if we continue to follow God's leading, we will make it through every obstacle and fulfill our purpose.

The Bible lets us know that Joseph's brothers did not like him at all because he was their father's favorite child. Moreover, they did not like him because he reported to their father when they were not tending the flock. Therefore, they hated him even more when he told them about the dream. When we know that someone does not like us or does not have our best interests in mind, we should have limited conversations with that person about the dreams and visions that God has given us.

A good example of this situation is seen when the adversaries of Judah and Benjamin found out that the children of Judah were going to build a temple unto the Lord. The adversaries tried to stop the work of God. Ezra 4:4–5a says, 4 *"Then the people of the land weakened the hands of the people of Judah, and troubled them in building,"* 5a *"And hired counsellors against them, to frustrate their purpose."* We must be protective of the visions and gifts that God gives us and not allow anyone to frustrate our plan and purpose. The devil will use people to stop what we are doing, but we must continue to focus on what God has told us to do and follow His leading.

Joseph's journey in life is an excellent example of trusting God, loving the Lord, and being obedient through hurt, pain, disappointment, false accusations, and prison sentences. Through all of this, he remained faithful to God. I have not read in the scriptures where he mumbled, grumbled, or complained. Joseph did not try to force his destiny. That is a lesson for us, we should not take God's matters into our own hands. We must continuously have our personal relationship fresh with the Lord. He will direct and guide us in His righteous path. Even when some things do not make sense, we must trust Him.

Sometimes we may walk through the valley of the shadow of death. We must not give up during these times, and we must not camp out in the valley. Furthermore, we should not be fearful because Jesus is with us, and He said that He would never leave us nor forsake us. God has given us His Word to speak to situations that may arise in our lives.

Now, for us to speak the Word, we must know the Word. Also, we must live the Word and expect a change, which may be instant. At other times, we may have to wait until the change is manifested in the physical realm. Jesus spoke the Word when he was in the wilderness being tempted by the devil in Matthew 4:4b. He says, *"It is written, Man shall not live by bread alone, but by every word that proceedeth out of the mouth of God." We must speak the Word of God to all of the negative situations that may come our way, using the authority that has been given to us from God.*

Getting back to Joseph, he was sold into slavery by his brothers to the Midianites, and the Midianites sold him to Potiphar. The Bible says in Genesis 39:2a, *"And the Lord was with Joseph, and he was a prosperous man."* This was when Joseph was serving in Potiphar's house. The Bible also says that Potiphar saw that the Lord was with Joseph and that the Lord made all that Joseph did to prosper in his hand, and Potiphar made him overseer of his house.

Can employers see the Lord in their employees today? Do they hear them talking about the Lord but not performing the duties on their jobs? Do these employees who slack on the job have the nerve to ask for a promotion and a raise? Joseph did not have to ask for a promotion. His work and the way he carried himself spoke for him. Even though Joseph was doing all the right things (and we can be doing the right things, also), some did not like him because he did not bend God's rules and do things as others saw fit.

A modern-day example is a millionaire who wants to build a top-of-the-line theater for the ministry that God has called me to oversee. The condition is that the millionaire may use two of the conference rooms twice a month for drinking, gambling, and other worldly activities. **The devil is a lie!** I would not accept that offer because it goes against the will of God. The Lord is my source. Now, if that millionaire wanted to build the theater or give me the money to have it done, with no strings attached, I would receive it and pray over it with thanksgiving and praises to my heavenly Father. I am sold out to Jesus. I know the devil's tricks, and I will not fall into his traps.

Continuing with the story of Joseph from the book of Genesis, Joseph was sold out to God when Mrs. Potiphar asked him every day to lie with her. He would not oblige her, so she grabbed his jacket as he ran away from her. Burning in her own lust, she became so angry with him that she lied and told her husband that Joseph had tried to rape her. Therefore, Potiphar had Joseph thrown in jail, which did not sway Joseph's faith in God. During Joseph's life, he stayed faithful to God. He waited and was not anxious to fulfill God's purpose for his life.

As Joseph walked in the wisdom of God, he was faithful in whatsoever he put his hands to do. He was not worried about how he was going to fulfill his God-given dream. He trusted God. When the dreams became a reality, Joseph was not arrogant, hostile, or bitter toward his brothers. When he saw them coming to buy food in Egypt many years after they had abandoned him, he recognized them. However, they did not know who he was. Joseph questioned them and discovered that his father and brother, Benjamin, were still alive. He gave them what they wanted and even more. Besides, he left their money in their bags. He also told them not to come back unless they had their younger brother with them.

The brothers had to go back to Egypt a second time for food, bringing Benjamin with them. Joseph had a meal prepared for them and had the servants leave the room. He made known to his brothers who he was. They were surprised and afraid at hearing this news, but Joseph was so glad to see them again, along with his baby brother. Joseph cried so loud that people outside the room heard him.

He asked his brothers not to be grieved or angry with themselves, and he explained his purpose to them. We see his words in Genesis 45:5–8a *"Now therefore be not grieved, nor angry with yourselves, that ye sold me hither: for God did send me before you to preserve life."* 6 *"For these two years hath the famine been in the land:*

*and yet there are five years, in the which there shall nei-
ther be earing nor harvest." 7 "And God sent me before
you to preserve you a posterity in the earth, and to save
your lives by a great deliverance." 8a "So now it was not
you that sent me hither."* Through all the ill-will that
the brothers had wished upon him, Joseph still blessed
them, and he never once blamed them. He told them
that God had sent him before them to save them, the
generations after them and other lives.

He had his brothers go and let his father know
that he was alive and wanted Israel (Jacob) and all of
his family to move to Egypt, and he was going to take
care of them. When Jacob's sons told him that Joseph
was alive in Egypt, he did not believe them, but when
he saw the wagon that Joseph had sent for him, his
spirit was revived, and he was ready to go to Egypt to
see his son.

Joseph was a very gifted man used by God to save
many people, including his own family. When God
gave Joseph those two dreams, Joseph did not know
how they would come to pass. He did not know all
the trials and tribulations that he would have to go
through. He endured being lied about, being hated,
being forgotten, and being in prison. Yet, he loved,
trusted, and obeyed God. Joseph saw his expected end,

and he loved his family, showed them compassion and took care of them.

When their father died, his brothers thought he would hate them and retaliate for the evil they had done to him when he was a child. That was not even on Joseph's mind. Look what it says in Genesis 50:18–21 18 *"And his brethren also went and fell down before his face; and they said, Behold, we be thy servants."* 19 *"And Joseph said unto them, fear not: For am I in the place of God?"* 20 *"But as for you, ye thought evil against me; but God meant it unto good, to bring to pass, as it is this day, to save much people alive."* 21 *"Now therefore fear ye not: I will nourish you, and your little ones. And he comforted them, and spake kindly unto them."*

Joseph told his brothers not to be fearful, he is where God wanted him, and as they thought evil against him, but God meant it for good. Just as Joseph did, we can and will fulfill the plan and purpose that God has laid out for us. While traveling on this journey, we will not know all the different changes that we will go through, but if we will continue to pray, trust, obey, and cast all of our cares over to the Lord, we will reach our expected end.

When Jesus delivered me and set me free from a lifestyle of drugs, alcohol, stealing, fornication, and adultery, I was free indeed, and I am still free today.

I never thought that I would be living a life with so much meaning. I give God the glory for all that He has done in my life and all the great things that He is still doing in my life. It will be an absolute joy when you find out the gifts that may be on the inside of you lying dormant, just waiting to be awakened. Why don't you ask God to show you what it is and wake it up! Be expecting and not doubting and start on the journey of your expected end.

God knows His plan that He has for you, to give you peace and fulfillment. Rest assured that you will accomplish all that He has called you to do. I say to those of you who already know what God has called you to do, walk in your calling, honoring God every step of the way. May you fulfill the plan and purpose that God has already laid out for you. Please remember: if God can use me, what about you?

If you are reading this book and do not know Jesus Christ in the pardon of your sins, there are sections later in this book that will help you make a quality decision and receive Jesus as your Lord and Savior. Always remember that the Lord loves you.

I am so thankful that God allowed me to yield to His calling, and I pray that what I have shared with you in this book will encourage you to live for Jesus to the fullest and fulfill the plan and purpose that God has for you.

May the peace of God always be with you all.

Scriptures on How Anyone can Receive Jesus in Their Life

*I*f you would like to receive Jesus Christ in your life, that would be the best life decision that you will ever make. It is really easy, but you must be true to yourself and true to God. Salvation is a gift from God, and the name of Jesus is the only name where by anyone can be save. The following scriptures clarifies how to receive salvation:

Romans 10:9–10, 13
9 "That if thou shalt confess with thy mouth the Lord Jesus, and shalt believe in thine heart that God hath raised him from the dead, thou shalt be saved."

10 *"For with the heart believeth unto righteousness; and with the mouth confession is made unto salvation."*

13 *"For whosoever shall call upon the name of the Lord shall be saved."*

A Prayer to Receive Jesus Christ as Your Lord and Savior

*D*ear Jesus, forgive me of all the wrong I have done. I believe that You are the Son of God, and I believe that God raised You from the dead. Your Word says that whosoever call upon Your name shall be saved. So, Jesus, I am calling on Your name. Save me and deliver me. I thank you. Devil, you have no right and no portion in my life anymore. I denounce you because Jesus is Lord of my life. Amen!

This is me (Teretha) when I was in elementary school.

The Reason We Need to Be Born Again

When God created Adam and Eve, there was no sin in mankind. The couple was in the Garden of Eden where they were not ashamed to walk around unclothed. In Genesis 2:17, God had told Adam, *"But of the tree of the Knowledge of good and evil, thou shall not eat of it: for in the day that thou eatest thereof thou shall surely die."*

The devil, working through the serpent, had a conversation with Eve and deceived her into eating from the tree of good and evil. The tree was in the midst of the garden, her husband was right there with her, he did not stop her, she even gave him some of the forbidden fruit and he did eat. Now God had told Adam not to eat of that tree, but he did. So, by Adam disobeying God, sin entered into the world. This biblical account can be found in Genesis Chapter 3.

Before the death, burial, and resurrection of Jesus Christ, once a year the priest would offer a bull or goat to cover his sins. He would do the same thing to cover the people's sins for one year. Year after year, this was done. The following scriptures give a description of this practice, then and now.

Hebrews 9:7, 11–14

7 "But into the second went the high priest alone once every year, not without blood, which he offered for himself, and for the errors of the people."

11 "But Christ being come an high priest of good things to come, by a greater and more perfect tabernacle, not made with hands, that is to say, not of this building;"

12 "Neither by the blood of goats and calves, but by his own blood he entered in once into the holy place, having obtained eternal redemption for us."

13 "For if the blood of bulls and of goats, and the ashes of an heifer sprinkling the unclean, sanctifieth to the purifying of the flesh."

14 "How much more shall the blood of Christ, who through the eternal Spirit offered himself without spot to God, purge your conscience from dead works to serve the living God?"

The understanding is that no more does the priest have to offer a yearly sacrifice for his sins and the people's sins. Jesus Christ became the final sacrifice, breaking down that middle wall of partition that was separating mankind from God. When John the Baptist saw Jesus coming to be baptized, he said, *"Behold the Lamb of God which taketh away the sins of the world,"* *John 1:29.*

Salvation for All the Choice Is Yours

God loved this world so much, that He gave His only begotten son. The following scriptures details this truth.

> **John 3:16–17**
> *16 "For God so loved the world, that he gave his only begotten Son, that whosoever believeth in him should not perish, but have everlasting life."*
>
> *17 "For God sent not his Son into the world to condemn the world; but that the world through him might be saved."*

When we receive Jesus in our lives after being born a second time, we will not have to die the second death. The following scriptures explain this in detail.

Revelation 20:14–15

14 *"And death and hell were cast into the lake of fire. This is the second death."*

15 *"And whosoever was not found written in the book of life was cast into the lake of fire."*

The Bible has a lot to say about hell and the lake of fire that will burn throughout eternity. We have a choice, and it is up to us to make the right decision. **I admonish you today, if you have not made the decision, please choose life by receiving Jesus as your Lord and Savior.**

Skits and Plays Written and Directed by Evangelist T. J. Lowe

On July 24, 2014, the play "When a Man Loves a Woman." Performed at Ron Robinson Theater was featured in the *Arkansas Democrat-Gazette* newspaper, Little Rock, AR, in the weekend section, "The Weekend Ten," the top ten things to do and places to be. We were number seven on the list.

On July 27, 2017, once again, our production was featured in "The Weekend Ten" for another one of our productions titled "I'm So Proud Of Being Loved By You." Performed at the Ron Robinson. We were number eight on the list for things to do.

On February 12, 2018, we had a Valentine's Dinner Theater event with a live stage production titled "A Love

Shake Up On Sweetwater Drive. Held at Maumelle Event Center in Maumelle AR.

On February 14, 2019, we had another Valentine's Dinner Theater event with a live stage production titled "A Love Shake Up At The Father's House. Held at Maumelle Event Center in Maumelle AR.

Skits

Get Real
Different Situations That Some Families Go Through
Are You Committed?
Samson and Delilah
I Love You
Bring Your Bags and Leave Your Baggage
Back to School
The Good Man

Plays

The Prodigal Daughter
The Devil's Supper
Is This Your Life
I Want to Get Married
The Modern Day Esther

What Do You Think About Yourself?
Unto Us a Child Is Born
The Great Passion of Jesus
The Black Hall of Fame
The Best Christmas I Ever Had
When a Man Loves a woman
The Prodigal Rededicates
I'm So Proud of Being Loved by You
Them Thare Church Folks
A Love Shake Up on Sweetwater Drive
A Love Shake Up at the Father's House
Sunny! What's Wrong With You?

There is more information on our ministry website: www.lujcm.org

The Lowes

Contact information: **Lifting Up Jesus Christ
Ministries P.O. Box 192452,
Little Rock, AR 72219 or**
Chaplainlowe@lujcm.org,
Evangelistlowe@lujcm.org